BEING BORN

BEING BORN

by

Frances Bruce Strain

APPLETON-CENTURY-CROFTS   NEW YORK

PRINTED IN THE UNITED STATES OF AMERICA

TO JOHN AND DAVID

CONTENTS

BEING BORN

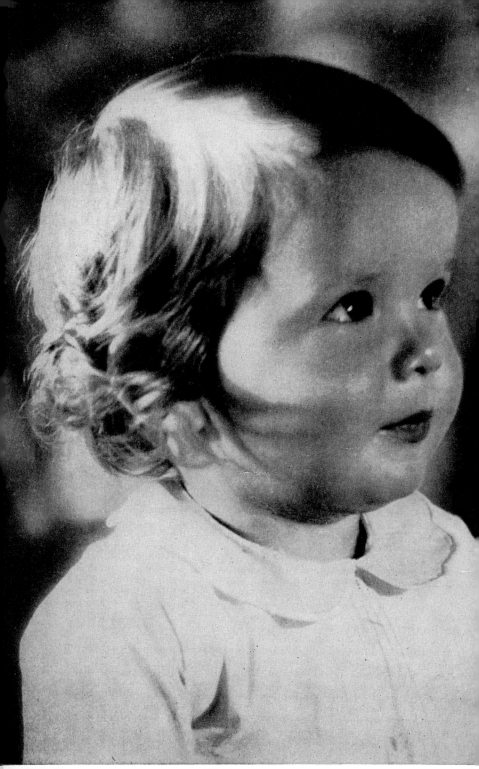

Under the microscope

WHEN one of the wise men of ancient times was asked to name the greatest event of his life he answered straightway, "Being born."

Of course! Come to think of it, being born is the greatest event of everybody's life. Otherwise, there would be no you, no me, no anybody to make things happen in this world of ours. But none of us remembers the day when he was born. We remember when we were six years old, perhaps, or five, or even four. We may remember our first sail on a boat, our first circus, or our first ride in an airplane. But not a thing about coming into this world do we remember. And, of course, nobody remembers anything that happened before he was born. We all should like to. Everyone has often wondered, Where was I before I was born?

It is a fairly long story. The answer to that question is long but fascinating, as fascinating as the story of *Treasure Island* or *Robinson Crusoe*. What is more, it is a true story, and even if we don't remember what happened, the adventure of coming into this world belongs to every one of us.

As you probably know, people live for the greater part of a year—for about nine months—before they are ever seen at all. They are growing and living inside of their mothers in a special place just made for them to grow in. During this period the mother is said to be *pregnant*.

In India, people get credit for these months of life before they are born. There are parties given in their honor and in honor of their mothers. So when they are born they have two birthdays, one after they started to grow all hidden away out of sight, and one when they came into the world. In India you could be ten years old and nine at the same time.

Embryos

During the period in the mother a person is just taking form. He is an unfinished person. He is not even a baby. He is called an *embryo*, and he doesn't look at all the way he is going to look when the parts such as eyes, nose, hands, and feet are ready with all the finishing touches put on.

You know what it is to model a swan or a squirrel from clay or a figure from a soap bar. Nature models her living things—swans, squirrels, boys and girls, everything—in much the same fashion. The great trick in Nature's modeling is that she makes her own stuff, or what might be called her modeling clay, as she goes along. She starts with a tiny particle of living substance and increases it millions and millions of times. The particle from which she starts this process is called a *cell*.

To see one of these cells you'd have to look at it under a microscope, one of those instruments like a magnifying glass, which makes it possible to see objects too small for our natural sight. The microscope is like several magnifying glasses arranged on top of one another, and instead of enlarging things a few times, it enlarges them several hundreds of times. Most cells are so very small that they must be magnified a hundred times or so before they look like anything at all. When properly prepared—stained with a dye—a cell looks like a small block, if it is square or oblong, or a very small marble, if it is round. A living cell itself doesn't look very exciting, just a clear, soft, jellyish substance with sometimes a little wall around it and always a thicker portion in the center, the *nucleus*. No, a cell isn't very exciting until you know what it can do. It may form a person. It may populate a world. It may make animals—elephants, tigers, lions, apes, horses, cows, every living thing upon the earth.

There are two kinds of cells, body cells and reproductive cells. Body cells are concerned with keeping people alive after they are born. They repair and replace worn-out or injured places. Watch the new cells set to work to repair the damage on a skinned knee or

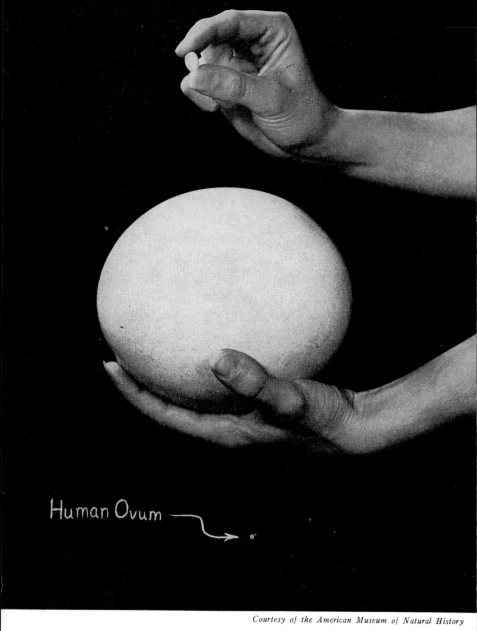

Human Ovum

Courtesy of the American Museum of Natural History

An ostrich egg compared to a tiny hummingbird's egg. (A human egg is much, much smaller still.)

cut finger. The reproductive cells have no concern with the particular individual to whom they belong; they are concerned with his descendants—future unborn beings. Their only task is to construct a new individual.

But to start somewhere. We all know it takes two parents to begin a family, a mother and a father. In women the reproductive cells are called egg cells; in men they are called sperm cells. One kind without the other is useless. In starting a baby the father is just as important as the mother. What's more, sperm cells and egg cells are just as different as men are different from women. Curiously, the egg cell or ovum is many, many times larger than the sperm cell. Being a lady, you would expect her to be smaller, but instead of being smaller, she is larger. She turns out to be the very largest cell of the whole body. That is saying a great deal when you realize that about twenty-six thousand billion cells go into our making. Twenty-six thousand billion, and the egg cell is the largest of them all. Yet she is tiny, scarcely big enough to be seen, about as big as the tiniest grain of sand. If you had right now two hundred egg cells and pushed them up close together in a row, the whole line of them would not measure more than an inch. Think how large you are now in comparison! Two hundred of you all in a row would reach clear across the gymnasium floor at school. As for an inch, it would not make so much as one little finger.

The sperm cell is much, much smaller than the egg. It is one of those marvelous unseen things which the microscope discovered. Sperms have round, flattish heads, no particular body, and tiny little whiplash tails which make them look like so many little tadpoles. Somebody has figured out that fifty thousand of them (fifty thousand persons is quite a city) could ride across the country on a United States postage stamp. So you see how very tiny they are.

The two cells shown are magnified reproductive cells as they might appear under a microscope. Slide I is an egg cell, or an ovum. And Slide II is a sperm cell. If you looked down through the microscope shaft at I, you would see something like the figure below. The

I

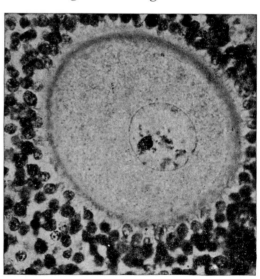

From the Carnegie Institution of Washington

A mature human ovum seen through a microscope and magnified 480 times.

dark spot in the center is the nucleus, the life-giving portion of the egg. If you looked down through at number II, you would see a sperm cell which is not much to look at, rather more like a polliwog than so serious an organism as a human life-giving cell.

Courtesy of Dr. R. S. Hotchkiss, New York Hospital

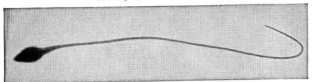

II

A sperm magnified 2100 times. The microscope makes it look as large as the ovum on the opposite page, but it is really much, much smaller.

If you look on page 42, at another magnified cell, this time a fertilized cell, you may see the very starting of the process which goes into the making of you or me, or any mammal, for that matter. Mammals, you know, are those who nurse their young with milk.

There you have them, egg and sperm, the makers of a world of people. Two invisible particles of matter to account for you and me, our fathers and mothers, our grandfathers and grandmothers, our friends, people of our race and other races for ages past and our children for ages to come. They are amazing, magical, incredible, elusive particles of matter, but they are *us!*

CHAPTER 2

Where the egg is made

IF ANYONE were to ask you where the various types of body cells were to be found, you'd have little difficulty in answering. Bone cells would be found in the bones of the head, arms, and legs, muscle cells would be found in the muscles, blood cells in the blood, and so on. Easy. But if someone were to ask where the reproductive cells, the creating cells, were to be found, you'd have to scratch your head and think. Boys would have their part of the answer more quickly than girls because they have known the place since they were very little. It is in plain sight, a little sac which hangs on the outside of them in the middle of the front, between the thighs. You will learn about it in the next chapter.

In girls the place where the egg cells are formed is on the inside, where it can't be seen. There are two places, really, that supply the egg cells, two compact little bodies called *ovaries,* each about as large as an almond and about that shape. Most all of us is made in two's: two eyes, two nostrils, two ears—one for a spare—so that if anything happens to one member, there is the second to help us out. The two little ovaries, one on each side, lie toward the back in the center and are inside a basket-shaped girdle of bone which protects the lower organs of the body between the hips. In girls the girdle is roomier than it is in boys, because when they become mothers, it must hold a good deal more—one baby, usually, and sometimes two, three, four, and even five babies.

The ovaries

While a girl is growing up, the ovaries are inactive. They are asleep and filled with a lot of drowsy little

A mother English setter taking her puppies for a walk.

Photograph by Harold M. Lambert

egg cells, hundreds of them. But when she becomes twelve or thirteen years old (sometimes younger, sometimes older), the sleeping cells begin to stir, stretch themselves, and make ready to leave their place. One by one they move out of the ovary into places where they can be found.

Just one egg cell gets ready at a time. When it does, it pops right through the ovary wall, leaving quite a gap behind it, which, however, is soon filled in. Then the egg cell is caught up by delicate waving hairs which draw it quickly into the trumpet-shaped end of a big tube. The tube isn't really large, no larger at its inner end than the inside of a pipe stem, but compared with the size of the egg cell it's a mammoth tunnel!

It takes about eight days for an egg cell to travel along the *Fallopian tube* before it reaches the inner end where it enters a roomy place about the size and shape of a pear standing stem end down. This is the place provided for babies to grow in. It is called the *uterus;* in the Bible it is spoken of as the *womb.* The uterus opens into a longer, narrower passage, the *vagina,* which leads to the outside of the body.

Suppose we stop for a moment here and draw the road map opposite. On it you may see the location of all the important places and passages in this journey of the egg cell.

No. I is the place where egg cells are formed, the *ovary.*
No. II is the tube that carries the egg cells away from the ovary, the *Fallopian tube.*

No. III is the sac in which the baby is to grow, the *uterus*.

No. IV is the passage that brings the baby into the world, the *vagina*.

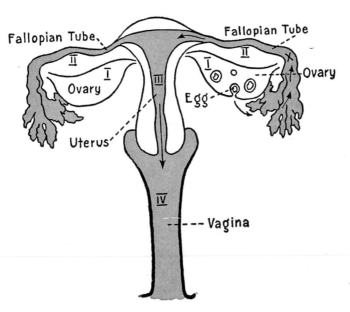

This map shows the mother's reproductive system.

When the ovary produces an egg cell, it does something else, too. It makes the lining of the uterus, the pear-shaped sac, all soft and ready for a new baby to nestle into and grow, just as we make a guest room in our home ready for an expected guest. Nature prepares the uterus by sending a generous supply of blood to fill up the network of blood vessels that wind in and out around the walls of the sac. The blood makes the lining easy for the tiny growing speck to cling to, and it provides food and oxygen for the little new person to feed upon as it grows. But most of the time there isn't to be any new person, because most of the time the egg cell isn't met by any sperm cell, so no new baby is started. The rich supply of Nature's food in the blood vessels isn't needed. The soft lining isn't needed either. Then what happens? Everything is discarded. The egg cell breaks up into particles and passes down through the opening and is lost. We don't know when, because it is too tiny for us to be aware of its passage. The walls of the blood vessels break down, too, and the unused blood comes trickling down through the opening and out of the body. As it comes, it carries with it fragments from the lining of the sac, the uterus. It takes several days for this bit of housekeeping to take place. Then it is past, and all is quiet again until the time when another little egg cell comes along.

Menstruation

The loss of the egg cell, the blood, and bits from the lining of the uterus are all a part of *menstruation*. You may not have heard the word. Many girls speak of it as their "period" because it occurs at intervals. All the time a girl is growing up and all through the years after she is grown up until she is forty-five or fifty years old, menstruation takes place about once a

A mother monkey comforts her child.

month. Only a few times it fails to occur normally, and that is when the sperm and egg have united and a little new person needs the warm, rich blood for his up-building. Yet menstruation can be and is as individual as are girls themselves.

But menstruation has a way of being delayed or missing altogether for many other reasons: poor health, worry over school examinations, any number of causes may interrupt the normal, even pattern of its course. During the first years of a young girl's matur-ing, irregularities are not unusual. The second period may be several months after the first one, or it may come on schedule about four weeks later. Nature gives her children time to adjust to the new and great changes that take place. If irregularities continue longer than a year or so, one should seek the advice of a physician, one who is specially trained.

Incidentally, men-stru-a-tion (such a long word and such a personal one for girls) usually abounds with nicknames: "sick period," "curse," "Aunt Mary"—all of them a bit, shall we say, flippant? "Ladies' Day" is a newcomer I've heard that just expresses it and is obviously entirely "ladylike."

Because there are so many things girls want to know about menstruation that do not belong to the story of the embryo, we have provided answers to the follow-ing questions:

I. How can you tell when menstruation is going to start?

There are various signs. Very often the breasts begin to grow larger and are tender to the touch. Occasionally there is a let-down feeling in the case of some girls. After the period is started, these girls feel much better, usually, and when it is finished, they feel as though they had been made over new. Many girls experience no special discomfort.

2. Why do some girls menstruate so much earlier than others?

Think a minute. Why are some girls taller than others, or heavier or quicker in their movements, or jollier or better company? Girls differ in the time and manner of menstruation just as they do in other things. It is a very individual affair. But there are some reasons back of the differences. In general, good health, good living all around, will tend to promote a normal sort of maturing; poor health, poor living conditions to delay it. Right now in many countries where living is unsettled, food scarce, one would expect to find the beginnings of maturity were delayed into later girlhood.

3. How long does it last?

Menstruation comes in periods. Each period lasts from three to five days, although it may be longer or shorter by a day or two in certain cases. The interval between the beginnings of two periods is about twenty-eight days or roughly a month. Many women speak of menstruation as their "monthly period."

4. Suppose it never did start, what would happen?

In some very rare instances women have not menstruated, but, even so, they are able to have children if the ovaries are discharging the egg cell. Menstruation is just an incident. The egg cell is the thing that is necessary. Yet if I were a girl and I had not begun to menstruate by the time I was, say, fifteen, I would go to a doctor and with my mother talk the matter over with him. Vitamins and hormones and good nourishing food, we know, can accomplish wonders when taken under direction.

5. Do you have to have cramps?

Of course not. Get rid of them as soon as you can. But the normally healthy girl usually does not have any pain at the menstrual period. Cramps usually mean congestion —that is, too much blood has filled into the blood vessels around the uterus and is pressing on the sensitive nerve endings. Becoming chilled by not dressing warmly enough or by sitting out for long periods in cold weather not properly protected will sometimes produce cramps. Keeping warm and not getting too tired, rubbing down well after a bath, exercising moderately and not to excess, are all good cramp preventers. If you should have pain, tuck up with a hot-water bottle or an electric pad. Take a hot drink and think of all the good fun coming. Gloomy thoughts are bad for cramps. But if pain persists, a few special exercises given by the school doctor or nurse might be just the thing.

6. What can a girl do during her period?

You mean, how much may she exercise? Quite a lot, much more than her mother was allowed to when she was a young girl. She may go to school, do light gym work, walk, dance in moderation, go to see a picture, and, in fact, do anything not too strenuous or tiring. Every girl must be her own guide, a guide with a conscience, too. We do not want her to think she can do what another girl can do; we want her to do what *she* can do with no bad results. An increase in the amount of discharge would mean, *Go slower!* Plenty of sleep and fresh air, not too much study, no worries, a little fun, the right amount of exercise, make a good program for the average girl at this time.

7. Can you take a bath and wash your hair?

Yes to both questions. The bath will be good for you— warm water in a warm room with a fine rubdown afterwards. But the caution against getting chilled must be observed. The reason our grandmothers didn't bathe during menstruation was because most of them had no nice warm bathroom, and there was plenty of chance to become chilled. The best rule is to take a daily bath or shower all through the month, including the menstrual period. The shampoo? Like the bath, present-day facilities make it a taken-for-granted procedure.

8. What is a sanitary pad?

It is a pad made of gauze and filled with an absorbent material. By attachment to a narrow belt at the back and the front, it is held in place and protects the clothing from the stain of the menstrual discharge. There are many such pads on the market, each with its own trade name, such as Kotex, Modess, Aimcee, and others. There are also tampons or "inserts" in addition to pads. These are little rolls of absorbent material about as big as your finger or smaller. They can be slipped up into the vagina quite comfortably when properly placed, and are especially convenient when dressing for swimming or dancing because they are entirely out of sight. Yet many doctors feel that tampons must be used with care and are not to be

depended upon for regular service. Yet in either case
(pads or tampons), they must not be neglected but
changed often to avoid a telltale odor. School nurses
always have a supply and there are "pocket editions" that
one may carry conveniently in one's purse to use in an
emergency.

9. What is the white discharge that comes?

There is a white discharge from the vagina that is called
leucorrhea. It often appears just before and just after
menstruation when congestion is present. Overwork, a
run-down condition, or worry is likely to increase it. Rest
and exercise in proper amounts, fresh air, and a happy
mind should do much to correct it. Any continuous discharge from the vagina except normal menstruation
should be referred to a physician. A discharge that is
yellow (not white) should be reported at once because it
would indicate an infection which needed medical care.

10. Why do they call it a sickness?

The term is left over from the days of our grandmothers,
when people looked upon menstruation as an illness. It
was not considered, as it is today, just one of the normal
activities of the body, like digesting food, for example.
Then, too, women had more pain because they dressed in
tight clothing and paid little attention to the laws of
health. For girls of today the word "sickness" does not
apply. With a little care for rules of health, menstruation
days can be just like other days, full of fun and good times.

11. Does it keep on all your life?

Not all your life. Usually a woman's menstruation periods continue until she is forty-five or fifty. Then they stop, and after that, of course, she has no more babies, for the ovaries that supply the egg cells have almost always shut up shop. They have finished their work. One might expect women to be glad when their menstrual periods were passed, but somehow, there often creeps in a regret at the thought there can be no more babies. No, there can be no more babies, but if there have been babies now grown up, there can be grandbabies to take their place. That helps.

CHAPTER 3

Where the sperm is made

Now for the place that makes the sperm cells. Suspended on the outside of a boy's body in a small sac of loose skin known as the *scrotum* are two intricate collections of little tubes called *testicles.* They hang right beneath the finger-shaped organ, the *penis,* which discharges the fluid waste of the body, the *urine.*

Along the inner length of these tubes the sperm cells begin to form when a boy is fourteen or fifteen. The tubes have a great length, greater than one would imagine—nearly a third of a mile if they were stretched out in a straight line. When you think that billions of sperm are formed at a time, you see why it is necessary that the tubes have such a length.

If one could look inside the bony girdle or *pelvis* of a boy, one would see the rest of his reproductive system. It is quite different from that of a girl. There is, for example, a tube into which all the tiny tubes of each testicle empty, very much as the tributaries of a

Fred Lewis from the National Audubon Society

Young kangaroos kissing.

river empty into the larger stream. This larger tube joins a second and still larger one which loops around inside the body in a big curve and then empties into a third tube which runs down through the penis to an opening at its tip.

Suppose we make another map to chart the region covered by all these tubes, a second road map which will show you where the sperm cells are to travel, just as we made a road map of the region that the egg cells travel. You will find the new map on the opposite page.

No. I are the tiny tube masses, the *testicles*.

No. II is the larger tube that gathers them into one stream, the *epididymis*.

No. III is the big tube that sweeps around in a curve, the *vas deferens*.

No. IV is the last one which discharges sperm cells, the *penis*.

During the years that a boy is growing up, the sperm-forming cells are drowsy and inactive, just as the egg cells are inactive in the ovaries of little girls. The larger tubes, too, have little to do, all but the one that discharges the fluid waste, the urine. The tube for that purpose operates in both boys and girls from the moment they are born.

Then, when a boy is thirteen or fourteen or fifteen, his reproductive system begins to stir and becomes active. The testicles get ready to make the sperm cells, and other places along the route of the larger tubes begin to make substances too. Together they form a milky-white or creamy-white substance which is called *semen,* or the *seminal fluid,* meaning a fluid that holds seeds or cells. Very often the fluid is stored in two sacs called the *seminal vesicles.*

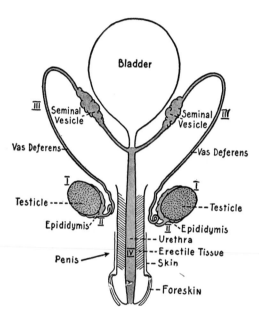

This map shows the father's reproductive system.

The ovaries make no fluid to carry the egg cell. There is no need. The egg cell is all by itself, fairly large in comparison, and does not leave the body while it is alive. It stays right under the shelter of its tunnel. The sperm cells, on the other hand, are formed thousands upon thousands at a time, are very tiny, and, what is more, they must leave the body of their maker to find the egg cell in another body. That is a real journey and a dangerous one. So Nature devised the seminal fluid. It holds the sperm together and acts as a carrier. In it they swim in a shoal like fish in a stream.

Some people are troubled by the thought that the seminal fluid must travel through the same tube that the urine passes through. It doesn't seem good planning to have a life-giving fluid and a dead waste product sharing the same passageway. They share, but not at the same time. Mother Nature is a good housekeeper and a good engineer. Whenever the seminal fluid is to pass along, she blocks off the urine in its bladder and keeps it blocked while the seminal fluid is passing through the canal. She does more. She sends out chemicals which make the passageway ready and destroy any acids that might injure the sperm cells. No, there's no possibility of collision in that system!

Boys observe that the two testicles are hung at different levels, one higher than the other, and that they hang differently under the influence of heat and cold—relaxed in summer, contracted in winter.

Sometimes at school one may notice a boy who has but one testicle showing. While baby boys are growing in their mothers, the testicles are caught up within the body wall; but about the time a baby boy is born, the testicles come down on each side through an opening in the tissues and hang suspended in the scrotum on the outside of the body. Once in a while they do not come down until after a baby is born. Now and then one does not descend at all. It stays up inside and is spoken of as an "undescended testicle." Sometimes the doctor will feel that treatment is advisable, sometimes not. As a matter of fact, it does not prevent the boy from growing up to be completely masculine and a good husband and father.

One may also notice at school a boy whose penis has no cap, or covering of skin, as well as one whose organ still has the cap or *foreskin.* All boy babies are born with the cap of skin, which acts as a protector, but many doctors think it should be shortened or cut away for hygienic reasons. People of the Jewish faith cut it away for religious reasons. The cutting is called *circumcision,* meaning a cutting all the way around.

Seminal emissions

During the early period when a boy is growing up and the seminal fluid is beginning to form, it quite frequently overflows at night, leaving a small quantity on the sheet or pajamas. If a boy is sleeping, he may awaken, and if he doesn't understand the experience, he may be frightened and disturbed. He has no cause for anxiety. The discharge is for him as normal as menstruation is for girls. It is to be expected, and it means that the time has come to grow up to be a man.

The following questions are often asked about this and other bodily processes:

1. How often does the boy's discharge of fluid come?

At irregular intervals. Sometimes it comes once in two months, sometimes once in three weeks, sometimes once in two weeks. It depends upon the individual.

2. How long does it last?

No time at all to speak of. The discharge comes at night when the boy is asleep. Often he is dreaming. Sometimes he awakens. In a second he is back asleep. It doesn't last through several days as menstruation does with girls.

3. Why does hair grow under the arms?

Hair increases on many parts of the body when the time comes to grow up—on head, eyebrows, legs, and arms. In both boys and girls hair appears under the arms and about the reproductive area. In boys, but not in girls, hair appears on the face and chest. Why does it come? Man is a mammal, and all mammals have hair on their bodies to a greater or less extent. Hair is a protection, and it is often an ornament. The lion's mane, for instance, not only protects his throat from the jaws of his enemy, but it makes him attractive to the lioness. Because human beings today use clothes as ornament and protection, bodily hair seems to be unnecessary. Hair on the head we still admire and cultivate.

4. How old does a boy have to be to be a father?

There isn't any given age. Usually the fluid that carries the sperm cells begins to form when a boy is fourteen or fifteen. At first it carries just a few sperm cells, possibly none at all that are of any value, but as he grows older, greater and greater numbers are formed. By the time a boy is seventeen or eighteen, he could, very likely, fertilize the egg cell. Some boys are virile or matured sufficiently to become fathers before that time. There is no way of telling without testing the seminal fluid.

5. Why are boys ashamed of the seminal emission, if it is all right?

They are ashamed of it only when they don't understand what it is or when they have been given wrong teaching. When boys know that the appearance of the seminal fluid is merely evidence that they are beginning to grow up, they feel quite different about it. They should feel very proud. Every boy wants to grow up to be virile and strong and take his man's place in the world.

6. What makes the penis grow hard?

The growing hard is called an *erection*. Usually the penis hangs limp and soft against the body. On different occasions Nature sends a quick supply of blood into the tissues or body substances of the penis which makes it become erect and hard. Very often on waking in the morning there is erection, possibly because the bladder has not been emptied of urine. Possibly for other reasons such as excitement over a ball game or fire, or over an examination, or punishment. When we are really stirred up, we get stirred up all over. For further discussion read page 30, Chapter 4, and Chapter IV in the book *Teen Days*, a companion to this one for older young people.

Two uniting cells

EVENTUALLY every-
one grows up. Eventually the time comes when these
two reproductive cells must find each other if they are
to carry out Nature's plan for a new generation. But
how? That is the question! The egg cell, of course,
must stay where it is, inside the mother, for that is the
place where the baby is to grow. After leaving the
ovary, you remember, it travels down the Fallopian
tube on its way to the uterus. Looking at the map on
page 11, you will see that the descending egg cell can
easily be reached by way of the connecting passages
from outside.

To the sperm falls the greater task of finding its
mate. It must leave the body of the father, enter the
mother, find the egg cell, and unite with it. Then there
are no longer two cells. There is just one cell, a *fertilized* cell, and from it the baby grows. You know the
word "fertile," which means able to produce. A fertile
field, for example, yields a rich harvest. Once the egg

A mother giraffe washing her child.

cell has been entered by a single sperm cell, the other thousands of sperm are warded off, and a protecting wall is formed about the egg.

The sperm cell not only starts the growth of the egg cell, but we believe it does two other things. It decides the matter of whether the new baby is to be a boy or a girl, and it gives some of the traits of the father to the baby so that he will be part like mother and part like father. These three things the sperm cell must do— just one sperm cell and no more.

Mating

Before fertilization comes *mating*. It is easy to confuse the two words. Fertilization is the coming together and uniting of the egg and the sperm, the two reproductive cells. Mating is the coming together and uniting of the father and mother, the carriers of the two reproductive cells.

When the two mates are ready to unite and the sperm fluid is to leave the father's body, the penis becomes hard and straight like a finger, though much larger in size. Erect, it enters more readily into the long narrow passage of the mother that leads up into the place where the egg may be found. Outwardly the father and mother lie close together, arms about each other, while the sperm-bearing fluid enters into the mother by way of the perfectly fitting passages.

In human beings this union between a man and a woman is called *coitus* or, more commonly, *inter-*

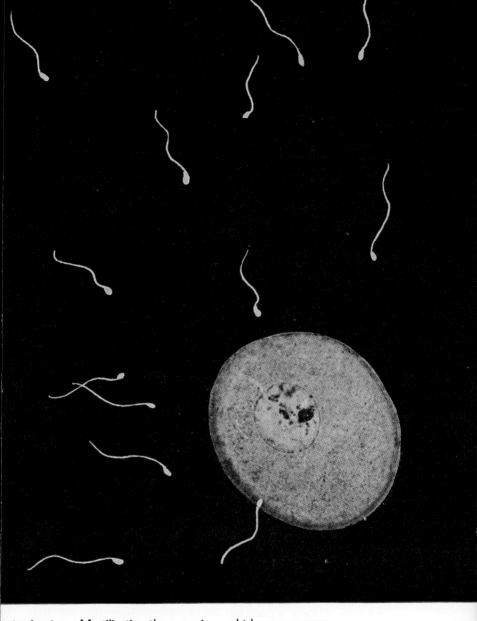

At the time of fertilization the ovum is sought by many sperm,
though only one reaches its goal.

course, which means an interchange, as one inter-
changes thought, feeling, friendship, or love with
another. Before mating, a man and a woman are drawn
together in a very special way. Usually they find and
choose each other out of many, many others. They
grow to love each other and to feel that they want to
belong to each other.

Because mating is not only a way to start one's
family, but is also a way of expressing their love, husbands and wives unite when no baby is to be started.
For many reasons, one cannot have all the babies one
might like, but one does go on loving. Mate loving is a
very special part of marriage and makes for happiness.

Because it is so intimate and personal a matter,
mating takes place in quiet and seclusion. No one is
allowed to observe it, for the presence of another person would spoil the deeper inner feeling.

Now you will want to know the answers to the following questions:

1. Is there any other way to start babies?

No, mating so far is the only way to start human babies
and animal babies. But not all creatures mate in the way
we have described. In many of the lower forms of life, the
female deposits masses of soft, jellyish eggs in water or
sand, and the male finds them and pours his sperm fluid
over them. Many of the eggs are fertilized, many are not.
Frogs practice an interesting kind of mating. When the
egg-laying season comes, the male frog swims up to a
female, climbs upon her back, clasps her around the

middle with his big front feet, and there remains until the moment comes when she shoots forth a stream of eggs from between her hind legs. At once the father sends forth his sperm fluid, which falls upon the eggs and fertilizes them. In both these cases many eggs are lost. By fertilizing the egg inside the body of the mother instead of outside, there is a great saving of life.

2. Can there be a baby if the father is dead?

Yes, many fathers have died without seeing their babies. It takes nine months for the baby to develop in the mother. Suppose the father and mother united and the baby were started on New Year's Day, and a month later the father died. The baby would still be his baby although it would not be born until October, eight months after his death.

3. How many times do the father and mother unite to start the baby?

It is difficult to say. If an egg cell is present in the Fallopian tube and live sperm enter the uterus, one of the sperm should be able to find the egg cell and fertilize it. It doesn't always, and if it doesn't, another mating must take place until one of the sperm does find and fertilize the egg cell.

4. Can you have as many children as you want?

The number of children one has is usually determined by several things—the mother's health, the father's ability to provide, and the conditions of one's life. Large families are usually happier families than small ones if health and comfort can be provided for all the members.

5. Do you have to have babies?

No, but most people want them. Marriage without children is not usually satisfying. But if a husband and wife decide they should not have children, then the sperm and egg cell must not be allowed to meet.

6. Can you have a baby if you aren't married?

Yes, one may have a baby though one is not married. There may be no husband, but there must always be someone who takes the place of the husband and is the baby's father. There has to be a father to supply the sperm cells and fertilize the egg cell; otherwise there would be no baby. A baby needs a father after he is born, too. He and his mother both need the father to love and care for them, to provide for them, and to give them a secure and I-belong-to-someone feeling in a home which bears his name. Mothers who do not have fathers for their babies lead a sorry life. Often the mother must work and leave her baby to the care of strangers and in changing homes. To ensure protection for mothers and their babies, society has formed certain laws and customs. One of these is the marriage vow which a man and woman repeat when they stand up before the world and pledge "to love, honor, and comfort" each other so long as both shall live.

7. I heard that the dark speck you see in an egg is part of the rooster. Is it?

The dark speck is the very beginning of the baby chick. It is the chick embryo. An egg with an embryo is a fertilized egg; one without it is an unfertilized egg. It could

never hatch out into a chick. For the egg to produce a
chick, a rooster and hen must mate, and the sperm find
the egg long before the shell has been formed about it,
and the hen has laid it in the nest.

A proud cocker spaniel mother with her new puppies.

CHAPTER 5

Three troops of working cells

UNTIL recently nobody had ever seen a human embryo from the very start. The smallest that had been seen was eleven days old and not larger than, well, just a speck. But today, in this age of wonders, an American scientist made an experiment that broke the record for seeing the earliest beginning of human life. He brought a newly discharged ovum and a new sperm cell together just at the proper moment (high fertility), put them tenderly in a test tube in his laboratory and was rewarded with the first known, first observed spark of human existence—the spark that starts the little you or me, the human embryo. This tiny baby lived but a few days, yet it served to show how each of us and the great world about us made their first beginnings.

Nothing in all the scientific world, not rockets or jets or deep sea craft, will draw the crowds like an exhibit of human life. At the Century of Progress Exposition in Chicago some years ago, there was a very fine ex-

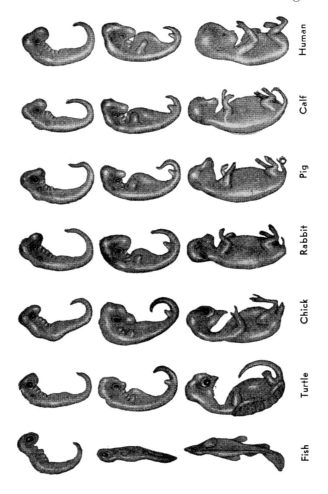

In the early stages all embryos, human and animal,
look alike.

hibit of embryo babies in all states of growth from the tiny specks up to the size they must be in order to be born. Crowds of people stood for hours before this row of bottled embryos—old men and young men, old women and young women, boys and girls of every age, climbing, stretching, jumping in their efforts to see over the heads of others.

What had happened to the babies? Why didn't they live? I can't tell you. Something went wrong. Possibly their mothers became ill and the embryos could not survive. At all events, they were preserved that more might be learned about them and the manner in which all human babies grow.

All kinds of embryos

In the early stages, that is, in the first few days of growth, all embryos—human, animal, bird, reptile—are much alike. Look at the collection of embryos on the page opposite and see if you can find yourself. Embryos? Are these embryos? Are these the beginnings of people and animals? They look like nothing so much as a lot of funny top-heavy question marks. They are question marks in a very real way, for you can't for the life of you tell chick from turtle, turtle from pig, pig from calf, calf from human. Cover up all but the first row and see if you can. It isn't very flattering to think you can't tell yourself from a pig or a turtle. The point is, they aren't yet pigs or turtles, but just the very beginnings of them, and much as they look alike, they couldn't be interchanged.

In the second row they are a puzzle, too. Their heads are bumpier and bigger, their fat little bellies stick out more than ever, the arms and legs have begun to sprout and look like stumpy little paddles. And every one of the embryos has a tail! Yes, even the one that is to be a human baby in the end!

In the third row every one is himself. The fish has his gills, the turtle his shell, the chick his beak and claws, the pig his snout and curly tail, the calf his hoofs, the rabbit his rapid foot, and the human baby his larger head for his larger brain, and his fingers and toes. Moreover, he has lost his tail.

If you have ever carved a boat from wood, you know yourself that at first it could be almost any kind of boat—a canoe, a sailboat, a rowboat, a launch—but after you had worked on it a while, it could only be the particular kind of boat you had decided to make. Or if you were modeling a deer, you'd have to start with a body, a head, four feet, and a tail, and that could be almost any animal. From the last stage shown in the picture on up to the time of birth all embryos take on the particular and special things that make them what they are going to be. They grow less and less alike and become more and more unlike.

One thing you must bear in mind: Most of these little animals are finished and born long before a human baby has even made a good start. Little pig is squealing his head off in his pen, the rabbit is nibbling cabbages in the garden, while you are still just an embryo. You take 280 days in the making—about nine months. A puppy takes about nine weeks. A kitten takes a little less, about eight weeks; a lamb, five months; a rabbit, four weeks; a rat, three weeks; a mouse, still less. Some animals take longer to make their babies than human mothers do. It takes ten months to make a calf, a year to make a colt, two years to make a baby elephant.

In general, the length of time required to make a living creature depends upon its size and its intelligence. Intelligent animals like the monkey family, elephant, and man have more complicated nervous systems; brain and spinal cord are more delicately geared. It takes a much shorter time, for instance, to make a kitten, which does very little beside catch mice, than it does to make a boy or girl who must go to school, learn to read, write, spell, become a doctor, lawyer, merchant, chief, keep a house, drive a car, manage a bank, or do any of the things men and women have to learn to do. So in general it takes a shorter time to make animals than it does to make human beings.

The difference between your modeling and Nature's is that you can change in the middle of things—you can turn your four legs, head, body, and tail into a cow, a horse, or a wolf at a moment's notice. But Nature's pattern is all set. It can't be changed. Each kind of animal reproduces only its own kind. From the very moment when an egg and a sperm meet, the pattern of the animal that is to be is made. It has to be the puppy or kitten or cub or chick or human baby that it started out to be, nothing else.

The next difference between Nature's work and ours is that Nature manufactures her own materials as she goes along. She has her one fertilized cell. She has her pattern. Then she sets to work.

Making cell material

Suppose we look into the workshop and watch just what happens from first to last. We'll put the microscope over a cell. It's a human cell. It is going to make a fine seven- or eight-pound baby in 280 days if all goes well.

To find this particular cell one would have to look in the Fallopian tube above where it enters the uterus. There is an X on your map that might be the place. If you could be watching at the time of fertilization, you

Cells increase by a process of division.

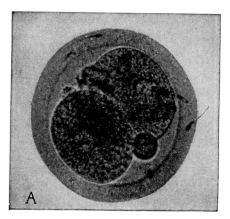
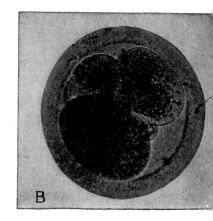

would see the head of the sperm plunge into the egg right through its thin wall. After this the living portions of the sperm and the egg fuse, so that there are no longer two cells, but one fertilized cell ready to set about its task of forming a new individual.

First this cell multiplies into hundreds of cells by a process called *cell division*. The original cell divides into two halves; the two daughter cells, as the halves are often called, divide again to make four. The four make eight, the eight, sixteen, thirty-two, sixty-four and so on, until in a very short time there is a solid mass of hundreds of cells clinging together like a bunch of grapes or a raspberry. You would think it looked like a golf ball. The cluster is often called the *mulberry stage* of the embryo. It doesn't look very promising, does it? Not like anything that could be developed into a boy or a girl! But just wait. Nature does not go on making human mulberries or blackberries forever.

If you could look into the ball at this point, you

After Lewis and Hartman, Contributions to Embryology, *Carnegie Institution, Washington*

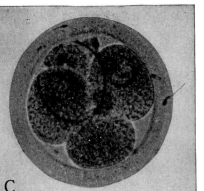
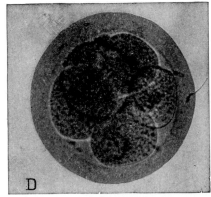

would notice that fluid had begun to form in the center, the ball had increased in size, and the cells had been pushed toward the outside of the sphere. Because the ball is now hollow, this stage of the embryo is called the *blastula* or *bladder stage*. When the blastula is well progressed, a mass of cells is formed at one point on the inner surface which arranges itself into a second layer. The two-layer stage is sometimes spoken of as the *gastrula* or *stomach stage* of the embryo. Later a third layer of cells is formed between the other two.

Special jobs for cells

These three sets of cells, the inner, the outer, and the middle layers, form the stuff out of which the various parts of the body are made. Nature gives to each of these layers its own job to do. Each layer specializes. The innermost layer makes those parts which are concerned with the feeding of the body—mouth, food canal, stomach, intestines, and the rest, commonly known as the *alimentary canal*. The middle layer makes the framework of the body. It has to be built around the very important alimentary canal, and it is built light so that the body may be moved about easily. Bone is light-weight material, hollow and porous. Bone makes the chest cavity, head, arms, legs, hands, feet—lots of things. That same layer makes muscle, too, to stretch upon the framework so that it is possible to move about in search of food, to reach and grasp it, and to escape from danger. We'd be pretty helpless without our muscles. There is also blood to be made, which feeds the bones and muscles, and provision for carrying off the waste left from the food that the body cannot use. The middle layer also makes the heart, the engine that sends the blood to all parts of the body with its load of nourishment. The middle layer has a man-sized job.

The outer layer has a very fussy series of jobs. It does the fancy work, puts on all the finishing touches: skin to cover the framework and muscles, hair, nails— in animals, hoofs and horns. This layer makes the nervous system and the sense organs—our eyes, ears, nose—those parts of us which let the outside world in to be seen, heard, smelled, and those other parts of the nervous system which let the inside of us, the real us, out. This nervous system with its lines and wires like a telephone system is a very difficult and fussy thing for the outer layer to make.

Once these three layers of cells are given their jobs to do, those jobs they do and no others. None of them shirks, and none changes its work. Not one of them says, "I'm tired making bones. I'd like to string nerves for a while." It can't be done, not at that stage of the game. So there we are. Science gives technical names to the three layers of cells: *ectoderm*—outside layer; *endoderm*—inside layer; *mesoderm*—middle layer.

These are the three great divisions of cells out of which Nature fashions her children.

CHAPTER 6

The baby workshop

ALTHOUGH the embryo has started to grow, the cell does not stay where fertilization took place. It continues its journey down the Fallopian tube just as an unfertilized egg does. This is necessary because the rapidly growing embryo needs roomier quarters. So it soon slips through the inner opening of the tube out into the pear-shaped sac, the uterus.

When you recall that the baby is to weigh seven or eight pounds before it is born, you might think that the uterus would soon be outgrown like last winter's coat. Not at all. The uterus is made so that it can expand to over five hundred times its original size. It is like a toy balloon that crinkles down and then blows up when filled with air; or it's like tough crepe paper that stretches endlessly. As the baby grows, his dwelling place grows too, larger and larger. It may even have to stretch large enough to hold more than one baby—twins sometimes, triplets, even quadruplets or quintuplets.

Where the baby grows

No sooner has the little human embryo arrived in its permanent home, the uterus, than it burrows into one of the deep folds of the crinkly lining. There it implants itself right in the wall, like a seed in the earth, and soon it is completely surrounded by two stout coverings or coats which Nature has built up around it. The coverings are like the high board fences that carpenters put up around a building in process of erection so that the come and go of daily affairs may do no damage to the new structure.

The outer covering or coat is a rather toughish one. It serves to attach the embryo to the wall of the uterus so that it may not easily be dislodged and have a great fall like Humpty Dumpty. The inner covering or coat is filled with a watery fluid. In it the embryo floats like a submarine while the water acts as a cushion, a water cushion, to save it from jolt or jar when the mother is walking or driving.

If the mother happens to be an animal such as a rabbit or deer or wolf, you can see that her babies would have much need for protection as she goes flying over the rocks and countryside trying to escape her enemies. A jolty journey such babies have.

How the baby is fed

In addition to the two coats which are built for the embryo's protection, there is another contrivance set up to bring it food, water and air until it can obtain them in the proper grown-up fashion outside. This

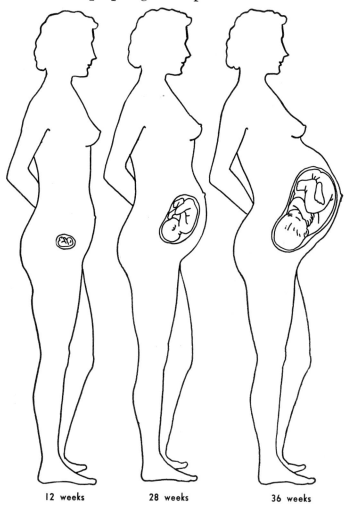

| 12 weeks | 28 weeks | 36 weeks |

The outline of the mother's body changes as the baby grows larger.

contrivance is called a *placenta*, which means a flat cake. In reality the cake is a mass of blood vessels belonging to both the baby and its mother and woven and interwoven into a flat mat against the inner surface of the uterus. As the walls of the blood vessels press close together, food, water, and oxygen from the mother's blood seep through into that of the baby and are carried to him through a little twisted vine of his blood vessels which connects him and his mother. With the embryo heart pumping busily 120 or more times a minute, the good food and oxygen are soon sent to all parts of the tiny body, ready to help it build more cells.

This mass of blood vessels, the placenta, is but a temporary convenience. It is like the scaffolding that carpenters put up to make possible the work on a building before it is finished. You've seen men climbing and walking on a framework of boards as they carry their bricks and mortar. After the building is finished, the workmen tear down this scaffolding. After a baby is born, Nature tears down the placenta and cord of blood vessels. If you will look in the middle of you, right in front, you'll see the place where the cord used to be attached. It's just a puckered little scar now, and it is called the *navel* or *umbilicus*. The cord is known as the *umbilical cord*.

In animals that have litters, such as dogs, the young are not developed in a central sac or uterus as human babies are, but in the branching tubes at the sides.

HOW ANIMALS REPRODUCE

FAMILY	NUMBER OF DAYS IN THE MOTHER	USUAL NUMBER OF YOUNG AT A TIME
Opossum	11	18
Mouse	22	10
Rat	22	10
Rabbit	30	6 to 8
Ferret	40	6 to 9
Guinea pig	62	2 to 6
Cat	63	4 to 6
Dog	63	6 to 8
Fox	63	5 to 8
Lion	110	2 to 4
Pig	120	10
Sheep	150	1 to 2
Goat	151	1 to 2
Tiger	154	2 to 5
Monkey	164	1
Baboon	169	1
Man	280	1
Cow	283	1
Horse	346	1
Seal	350	1
Walrus	365	1
Camel	395	1
Elephant	600	1

From *Life in the Making* by Alan Frank Guttmacher, by permission of The Viking Press.

These tubes are larger and heavier than the human Fallopian tubes. They are more like a double uterus, or twin sacs with the vagina a third sac or passage lying between. When you think how many puppies or kittens a mother animal can have—six, eight, or twelve —you realize that they could not all grow in one little place. The whole thing (tubes and uterus proper) looks like a letter Y. The puppies lie curled up in the upper branching forks.

When it is time for them to be born, they are pushed one by one into the lower tube and so out into the world, much as human babies are. If you have seen a mother dog or cat about to give birth to pups or kittens, you may have noticed how she rounds out on both sides where they lie curled up in the tubes. Human mothers round out in front because their babies grow in the central position.

In birds, the hen for instance, there is no sac or uterus. The eggs develop in a mass in the body cavity and are carried down to the outside of the body through the *oviduct*, a name derived from the Latin which means egg tube (*ovum*, singular, and *ova*, plural, for egg, and *duct* meaning tube or canal).

Sometime when your mother is preparing a hen for Sunday dinner, ask her to let you see the hen's reproductive system. You will notice, probably, a mass of tiny eggs (*ova*)—hundreds of them clinging together about the single ovary. Look at the multitude of transparent little dots almost too small to see and all the others ranging in size up to large yellow yolks.

It takes, roughly speaking, from ten to fourteen days for one of the tiny eggs to develop enough yolk to permit it to drop of its own weight into the funnel of the *oviduct,* as the tube is called which carries the egg to the outside.

When a young hen or pullet is about four months old, one yolk drops down into the oviduct about every

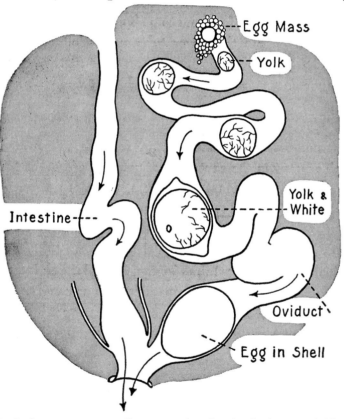

Each day a new egg yolk is started and a finished egg is laid in the nest.

twenty-four hours, so that each egg is about a day behind its predecessor during her laying period.

The yolk, which in a fertilized egg carries the embryo on its surface, is the food of the chick for the period of its growth before hatching and for a short time after hatching. The white, which forms about the yolk while the egg is descending the tube, supplies the building material of the chick's body—its feet, wings, feathers. The shell is formed later, just before the egg is laid in the nest—a light, porous protective covering for the whole until it is time for the chick to hatch out twenty-one days later.

When the time comes for the baby chick to peck its way out of the shell, he doesn't get frightened and strike aimlessly in all directions. Instead, he sets to work systematically and pecks in a very orderly fashion around the shell, so that at last it falls apart in two fairly equal halves.

If the baby chick is having trouble with his pecking, the mother hen will know it by the sounds and come to his rescue. One or two quick stabs with her sharp bill will do the work. At first the baby chicks are all wet from the fluid that has surrounded them in the shell, but in no time at all they are dry and all fluffed up into yellow balls.

If you will compare these baby workshops, you will see that the neatest and most complete of them all is the one in which Nature makes her human babies.

CHAPTER 7

From embryo to baby

MANY interesting things go on inside the protecting coverings of the baby during the nine months he is hidden from sight in the mother. After the stage when the three layers of cells are formed, work goes ahead at a rapid pace.

Third week

By the end of twenty-one days, if you had your magnifying glass at hand, you would be looking at the little question-mark embryo such as you saw in the illustration on page 38. You would not know that it was a human embryo unless you knew that it came from a human mother.

Fifth week

At the end of thirty-five days the embryo is about a fifth of an inch long. That would be about as large as a grain of rice. If you could hold this little grain-of-rice baby in your hand, you would find it had a little beating heart, far-apart eyes, stumpy little paddles of hands and feet, and the very first traces of the parts that go to make a boy a boy and a girl a girl. But at this time you could not tell whether it was to be a boy or a girl because at the very beginning these organs of both are alike. There is a tail, too, at this stage, not a round dog tail or mouse tail, but a flat, fishy kind of tail. One doesn't stop to worry about these early looks of the embryo, however, because it changes so rapidly and we are confident of what the final result is going to be.

Eighth week

As the end of the second month approaches, you would see many changes. The embryo is now all of an inch long! He has eyes, ears, hands, and feet, but they are not all finished off. The eyelids are closed over far-apart eyes and sealed tight together. The ears are just pits, as they are in some seals. The tiny, curly outer ear, the part that is intended to help catch sound waves, has not yet started. The arms are no longer stiff little paddles. They have three parts, upper arm, forearm, and hand. On the hand you can see the first faint markings of the tiny fingers. You wouldn't like the looks of this baby. It isn't at all pretty. His head is huge—about the same size as his body—and quite square, as though he had been packed in a tight box and got well flattened against its sides! Because his body is so small, he can't hold up his big box of a head, so you would

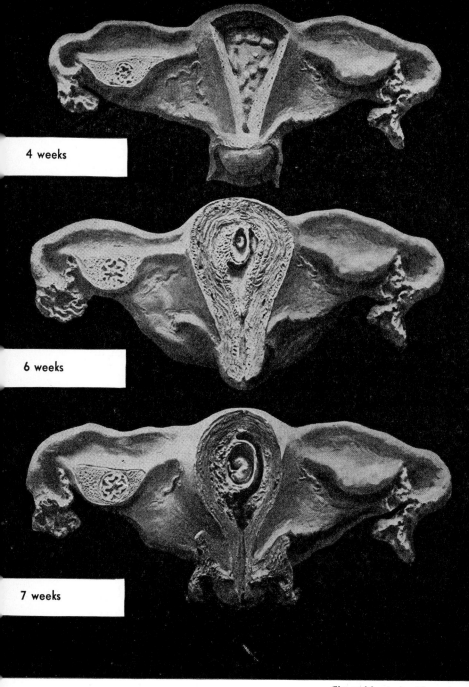

4 weeks

6 weeks

7 weeks

*Clay models reproduced by courtesy
of Maternity Center Association*

The embryo grows rapidly during the first weeks.

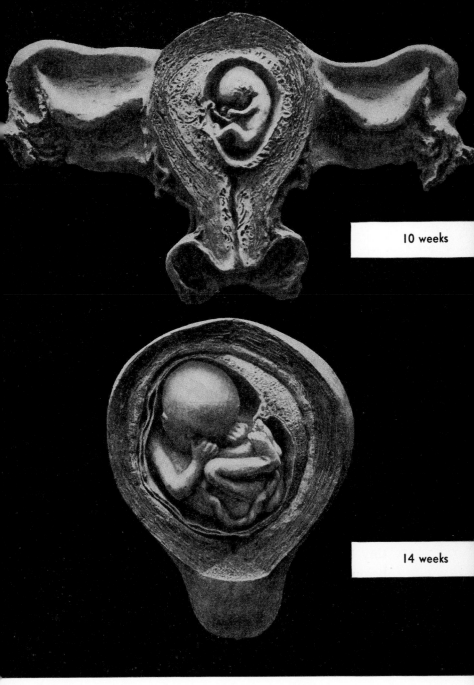

10 weeks

14 weeks

Courtesy of Maternity Center Association

By the fourteenth week the embryo looks like a real baby.

find it toppled forward. He is still not at all beautiful as you expect a baby to be.

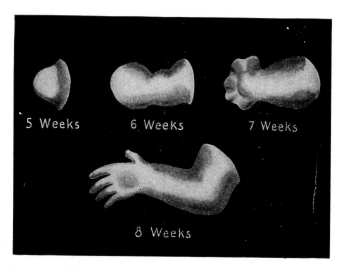

Hands and feet blossom from tiny buds.

Twelfth week

At the end of the third month you would see a very promising baby embryo between three and four inches long. His head is beginning to straighten up, and it is not as oversized and boxy-looking as it was. The fingers are tiny, perfect little fingers, and the feet have tiny toes, and tender, transparent dots of nails have begun to grow. Because the soles of the feet face each other, an embryo baby could clap with his feet as well as with his hands, or play "pat-a-cake" with both hands and feet. A newborn baby could, too, for that matter, if he knew what was expected of him. Best of all, at this period you can tell whether the embryo is to be a boy or a girl. Outwardly he looks quite complete even though he is no longer than your finger. It amazes you!

Sixteenth week

Graduation time has come. The baby has stepped out of the embryo class, the kindergarten, and gone into the *fetus* class. There he stays until the time comes for him to be born. And there he grows, becoming more and more like a real person every day. He is now quite sizable, about seven inches from top to toe. In the lower illustration on page 57 he looks all folded up like a jack-in-the-box. But he is not so folded as he looks. He moves about in much the same way that he does later when he is lying in his crib. Mother can tell you, for every once in a while he gives a little kick inside of her, which at first feels like the flutter of a bird in the hand. She likes the feeling—if it isn't too strong—for it's his way of telling her he is safe and sound and soon will be ready to be born. The Bible calls these movements "quickening."

As the baby grows stronger, his movements become more vigorous. If you should put your hand against his mother's side, you could easily feel the baby's stirrings. Often he makes a little hump that you can see. Babies do all sorts of things in that little hidden-away place of theirs. They sleep and exercise and rest. You can also hear the little heart beat if you put your head down close to the mother's side and listen carefully. It is also said you can hear them hiccough. They can't cry because their lungs have not begun to work yet. They have nothing to cry with.

Twentieth week

Strangest of all, the baby in his fifth month has begun to grow all over himself a fuzzy, soft, hairy coat. All mammals have hair over them at some time in their lives, but humans lose it before they are born. Dogs, horses, wolves, lions, most other animals keep theirs, and as they grow up, it becomes heavier and longer.

Baby bear cubs and baby rats and mice are born naked but soon acquire a thick, heavy coat. Elephant babies, on the other hand, are born with a fuzzy coat but discard it later for a tough hide with just a few wispy hairs scattered here and there, which makes them look like bald-headed old men.

Once in a great, great while, the soft, downy coat on a human being does not disappear. It stays. Then, when he grows up, some circus pays him a good price to be exhibited before the public as the Wild Man or Wolf Man.

Most babies have a little hair on their heads when they are born, and also eyebrows and eyelashes. As they grow older, bodily hair will increase, but only in certain places, as on legs and arms—not all over the body as before.

Twenty-fifth week

In about four more weeks, at the end of the sixth month, the baby measures ten to eleven inches long, and his eyes are opened. That is a big step forward. Puppies, kittens, rabbits, mice, still have their eyelids closed when they are born. But they are not blind; one must not try to force their eyelids open, but let Nature take her time about the matter.

This sixth-month baby is a very wrinkled baby. He looks like a little old elf. Sometimes he is still wrinkled when he is born, but he soon fills out as a little fat gathers under his skin. Many babies fill out round and smooth before they are born. If a baby were born at the end of this period, the sixth month, he might live only a few minutes, but if he were put into a modern incubator he might be saved to grow up like other babies.

Thirtieth week

A baby born at the end of the seventh month has a much better chance of growing up if he is well cared for. The closer a baby comes to remaining his full term of 280 days in his mother, the better are his chances of living. So seven months is a milestone in his behind-the-scenes career. At this period he is about fourteen inches long and may weigh as much as two or two and a half pounds. He is much better-looking than he was. His nose has begun to take form, his jaw is bigger and

doesn't hide away under his chin as it did. His finger-
nails and toenails are finished.

Thirty-fourth week

To most babies the next month brings still more fat
under the wrinkled skin. The baby's vital organs, the
lungs and stomach that he must have to live a life of
his own, are all polished off and ready to set in motion
like a new automobile. The soft hairy coat has disap-
peared. This baby weighs about five pounds or more
and is fourteen or fifteen inches long. If he were born
at this time, he would have an even better chance of
life than the seven-month baby would have, because
he is just so much nearer completion. What is more,
you'd see a real, sure-enough little person—no embryo
or fetus about him.

So the modeling goes on, a little more and a little
more each day, until a delicate piece of machinery, a
human baby, is ready to be launched into the world.

Here are some more things you will want to know:

1. Can you choose what kind of a baby you want, boy or girl?

Many people would like to, but Nature does not permit
it. We would soon throw her system all out of balance.
There soon would be too many of one kind, too many
boys or too many girls. Then when mating time came, a
large number would be left without mates.

2. What makes some babies boys and some girls?

The sex of the baby, whether it is a boy or a girl, is

thought to be determined by something in the sperm cell called a *chromosome.* Many believe that there are two kinds of sperm, one containing the X chromosome which makes boy babies and the other the Y chromosome which makes girl babies. It is purely a matter of chance which kind of sperm fertilizes the egg cell in the mother. A longer explanation in *Teen Days,* Chapter VI, page 73, may make this clearer.

3. Can you tell beforehand whether the baby is to be a boy or a girl?

No, babies are surprises. Sometimes the doctor tries to tell by listening to the rapidity of the little heartbeat, but this method is largely guesswork. One doesn't really know until the baby is born whether it is a boy or a girl.

4. How does the mother know that a baby is started?

There are various signs. Sometimes the breasts commence to grow large and are tender because they are beginning to get ready to supply milk for the baby after he is born. Some mothers are a bit dizzy at times, or grow faint. Sometimes the stomach is a bit disturbed during the first few weeks. Often there is no other sign at first except that the menstrual periods stop.

5. Does she have to tell the father, or does he know about the baby's coming?

She has to tell him. Husbands and wives know, of course, that they have united, but the sperm cell does not always find the egg cell. The mother herself doesn't always definitely know until she feels the baby moving about. That is a sure indication.

CHAPTER 8

Coming into the world

THE END of the ninth month! That is a time of rejoicing, for the baby is ready to be born. He weighs all of seven pounds, sometimes eight, even nine or—once in a while—ten whole pounds! He takes up so much room that he completely fills the uterus, that crinkled pear-shaped sac which has stretched out so amazingly as he grew.

Then one day the muscles of the uterus contract in preparation for starting the baby on his way into the world. At first the muscles contract gently and at long intervals, so that the baby and his mother have long periods of rest between. Gradually they press stronger and stronger and more and more frequently, until at last there is a churning and pressing that break the two stout coverings that have kept the baby secure in his mother. The water sac bursts and lets out a rush of water, just as a paper bag bursts and lets out the air when you have blown it up and popped it. Out comes the baby, too, and because the fluid has trickled down and oiled the way a bit, he slips through the narrow neck of the uterus more easily and down the second passage out into the waiting doctor's hands.

Doesn't the pressing and pushing hurt the baby? I suppose it does, poor mite, but Nature helps by providing the soft spot, the *fontanelle*.

The soft spot

If you could put your hand on a newborn baby's head, you would feel a soft spot, and you could see it rise and fall with the beating of his little heart. When a baby is ready to be born, Nature has finished him all off, lungs for breathing, stomach for digesting food, ears for hearing—all but the head. That is left unfinished, for it has a job to do. The head's job is to lead the way down the passage when the baby is being born. The bones of a baby's head before he is born are separate structures, with soft membranous spaces between their margins called *sutures*. The irregular spaces formed by the intersection of two or more sutures are called *fontanelles*. When a baby's head comes down through the birth canal, the soft membranous spaces between the separate bones permit it to be compressed to a considerable extent, so that the baby's head becomes much smaller without injury. After he is born, the bony growth of the skull gradually fills in the open spaces until they are closed. That is a wonderful device of Nature's which has saved many a little head.

Animals are usually in quite a different position when they are born. Instead of coming down the birth canal with the head foremost, as in the case of human babies, they present first the two fore feet with the head lying flat between them.

The afterbirth

After the baby is born, there are more churnings and contractions of the muscles of the uterus, and out come the two wrappings and the placenta, the *afterbirth* as it is called. The temporary structure has done its work, and it is disposed of as soon as the doctor cuts the cord that attaches the placenta to the baby and ties it close to the baby's body. Gradually the place where the cord left the baby's body heals over, and all that remains is the little, puckered navel.

Animal mothers are their own nurses, doctors, hospitals, all rolled into one, and they take care of many difficult situations. Many puppies come each wrapped up with his own placenta, like a chestnut in its outer burr. One by one the mother dog will break the sac and nose them out of their coverings, for they would smother if left long without air. After an animal baby is born, the mother usually bites off the cord that attaches him to the placenta and to her. Then, instead of burying the placenta as we would expect her to do, she eats it. It is said to be just what her system requires.

To us this seems—well, not a very dainty diet. Perhaps it isn't, but it is good housekeeping and serves to keep the animal neat, tidy, and clean. More than this, each animal mother licks and scrubs her new babies until they are as clean and shining as any human baby fresh from its nurse's hands.

But to return to human affairs. Most babies come crying into the world. They give a tiny, wee, wailing kind of cry—without tears, but just the faint sounds that are made as the air rushes for the first time into the little new lungs. Sometimes, if he doesn't commence to breathe properly, the baby gets a little slap on the back to start him off or at most a twirl by his feet to force the air into him. For the most part there is no difficulty at all. But once in a while there has been, and many a doctor has blown his own breath into a baby's mouth to start the breathing. Today's science has provided doctors with a little pump called an inhalator which can prime the baby's lungs into action in time of need.

It takes varying lengths of time to bring a baby into the world, and it is a different experience for each baby and each mother. A first baby usually requires longer than a second baby or a third, because the mother's organs do not respond as quickly as they do after the passages have been made larger and have had more exercise. A first baby takes on an average seventeen hours to be born, a second baby about eleven hours. Some babies take more time, some take less.

Pains and worries

Once in a while one hears some disturbing stories about the pain of childbirth. They make you think, "I don't believe I shall want any babies when I grow up.' You are worried if mother is due to go to the hospital for a little new baby brother or sister. The disturbing stories got started long ago when there were no hospitals, no doctors, no nurses who were especially trained in the care of mothers. It is labor, hard labor, to bring a baby into the world; indeed, that is what

Here is the fully formed baby, just before being born.

Courtesy of Maternity Center Association

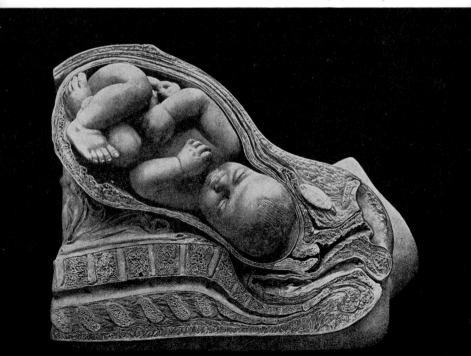

the process is called, *labor*. But look what the mother gets for her work. Isn't the lovely baby worth it?

Besides, you must always remember that labor pains are natural pains, to a certain extent, and come from natural causes—although increased, perhaps, by our civilized world habits which make people a little less hardy. They are not like the pains that come from an automobile accident when a person has been shot into the air or down a cliff. No living body was intended to be given that treatment. But women were meant to have children: their bodies were made for it and they are usually better when they have fulfilled their purpose if they are well and strong. Labor pains are

As the head emerges the doctor takes it in his hands to help the baby on his way.

Courtesy of Maternity Center Association

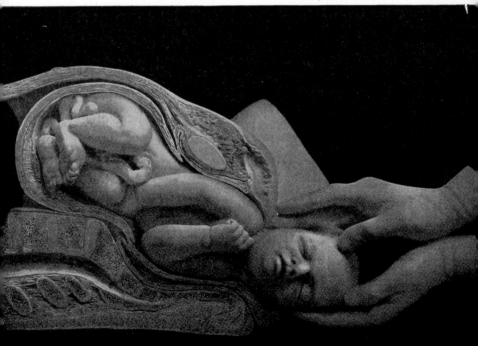

caused by the contractions of the muscles which push the baby down the birth canal—muscles, by the way, which are new at the job for first-time mothers and have never been used for this purpose. But they are strong and powerful, the strongest in the human body.

Also, labor pains are not continuous pains. They come in a series at regular intervals, with long periods of rest between. At first, the pains are likely to be short and sharp. That gives warning that the time has come for the baby to arrive. During the intervals of rest, mother gets her belongings together, calls the doctor and makes ready for her trip to the hospital. In many hospitals, some sort of anesthesia (pain-reducing medicine) is usually given to mothers when they enter. It is routine like your cold or diphtheria shots at school.

Yet all babies are not delivered routinely. Some mothers want to see their babies born, some want to see the whole process, some would rather go to sleep and wake up when all is over.

Much has been written about "natural childbirth." It is a method which relies little, if any, upon anesthetics, and gives a mother her full share of helping bring her babies into the world. During the months of waiting she is learning every step of the process—what is to be expected of her at each point of the baby's descent, and is practicing a lot of limbering-up exercises with other mothers who all look like a row of runners on the school track just ready to take off as they take their positions. Like the runners, these young

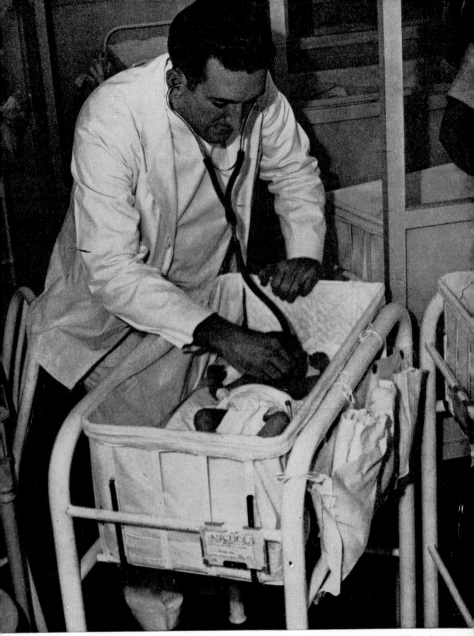

Soon after birth the baby is carefully examined by a doctor.

mothers go to the hospital to work and win with little thought of worries when the great day arrives. Natural birth is very challenging and reminds one of very early days when there were no doctors, no hospitals—but courageous mothers and plenty of babies. Yet even in natural birth today, the doctors and the hospital's services always stand ready to help in time of need.

The opposite of natural birth is called a Caesarian (pronounced See-zair-i-an), or surgical birth. In this case, a mother takes no part in the delivery. Perhaps you have seen a long white scar on your mother's abdomen and asked, "What made it?"

Laughing, mother may say, "You did!"—and then explain.

Caesarian births are not frequent—about one in several thousand is the record. But they make it possible for some mothers to have babies that otherwise couldn't have them. Certainly, they are much easier on the baby. He gets lifted out through an opening made in the abdomen rather than being pushed and shoved down the birth canal. When the time comes, the mother is put to sleep, the doctor makes a long cut (incision) just over the place where the baby is waiting, fastens back the sides of the body walls (as you fasten back the sides of a pup tent) and lifts the baby out. It is all over in a few minutes and for most of these mothers it is the only way. The doctor usually decides when Caesarians are necessary.

Sometimes the doctor thinks it best to help by shifting the baby's position so that he can make better progress, and sometimes he slips a shining instrument around the baby's head and gives him a lift out. Babies so delivered are called "instrument babies." The lift does not hurt them in the slightest if a careful doctor does the lifting. It helps both the baby and his mother.

In many hospitals mothers and babies are cared for separately, the babies in a big glass-walled nursery where each new baby joins a crop of other new babies

Friends and relatives can see the baby in the nursery, though he is separated from them by glass to protect him from any germs.

N. Y. Daily News—*Gilloon Agency*

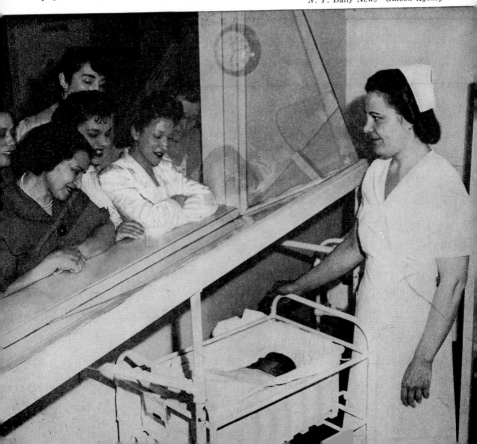

in his little plastic basket on wheels, each just so far
and no farther from his neighbor like a regiment of
soldiers on parade. Each little fellow, too, has his
locker at hand, a little cabinet filled with his personal
necessities: sheets, gowns, diapers, every toilet re-
quirement. There, in those transparent little beds, the
babies sleep through their first days of life. Which will
you have?—the little redhead, the big husky, the one
with his fists in his eyes? It's all very impressive, even
thrilling, but if one of them is your own baby in there
which you would like to get hold of, you feel the way
you do when standing before a candy store window
and you are not allowed to go in and buy something.

Mothers often stay in a large room called commonly
a "maternity ward" with other mothers in rows of
grown-up single beds which can be separated by mov-
able screens for privacy's sake.

The visit to the hospital is often a gala occasion for
the mother. She can look forward to a most beautiful
rest after the baby is born, with little to do but sleep
and read and wait for a jolly young nurse to bring trays
full of good things to eat. Between times there are
flowers arriving, and gifts and letters. Every now and
then, at regular intervals, the little new baby comes in
for some food of his own. Best of all, she has special
evening and Sunday visits from father who is often the
only favored one allowed to see her. Not even grandmother is permitted, and in some hospitals, neither
friends nor telephone calls.

There was a time when fathers themselves felt they were outsiders in a maternity ward. Today, they are considered an important part of the whole occasion— a great help and comfort. Their big strong hands are good to hold onto when little Mr. Baby is pressing too hard on his way down the birth canal before delivery, as mother is waiting.

Later, when the time comes for mother to go into the delivery room, father joins the group of other waiting fathers in a little lounge sometimes called "The Stork Club," where they all keep each other company, but with an eye on the door for the nurse in charge who comes to report the good news to each father in turn. Happy is the man whose turn comes, for he may be escorted down to the delivery room and, all dressed up in white hospital coat and cap, allowed to greet wife and baby and claim them as his own!

It is a memorable occasion, like becoming a United States citizen. Then and there, the baby is tagged with the name that settles this small person's identity for keeps. Sometimes, the babies are tagged with a piece of adhesive, like a name tape, stuck upon their little backs. And in some hospitals, a necklace or bracelet made up of a string of beads which spell the baby's name is used.

In many hospitals, the babies are fingerprinted. The nurse holds the little hand or foot to an inky surface and there it is ready for the record. So many mothers want the printings for their baby books, some hospitals prepare special certificates all signed and sealed with them for departing babies.

Not all babies are cared for in the big hospital nurseries or their mothers in the maternity ward. A few mothers are able to secure private rooms which makes it possible to have their babies with them night and day as though they were at home. This "rooming in" plan (funny name—as though a baby were a boarder) is a specially nice arrangement. Many mothers choose it and love it. It does away with that "where is my baby gone?" feeling on their part and it does much for the baby, too. Not only his little stomach gets fed, but his spirit as well, when close to mother in his little "glass bed," he awakens each time to the touch of her loving, welcoming presence.

On page 81 see how happy everybody looks. The baby's bed is swung across mother's; the sides are let down like the sides of a showcase to allow easy care. At the side is a tall locker, as in the outer nursery, full of his belongings: blankets, nighties, diapers—all right at hand for mother to use.

Formerly, the doctors required their patients to stay two weeks in the hospital. They thought it required that length of time for the reproductive machinery to get back to normal after its heavy work. Today, most mothers are allowed to return home at the end of a few days—about five as an average. Once at home, they are put to bed and required to rest until little by little they are able to return to their daily duties.

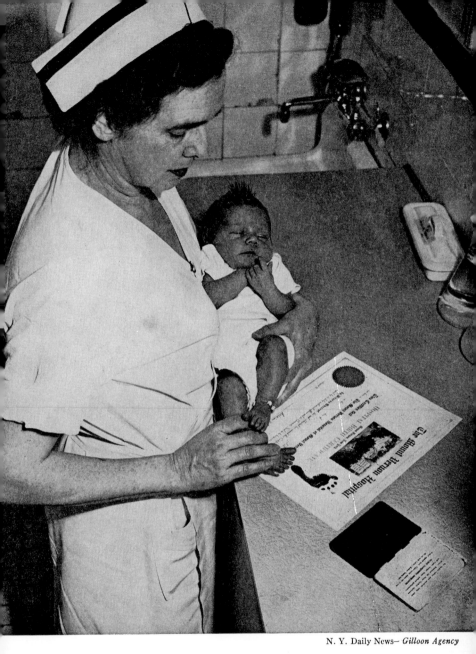

A nurse takes the baby's footprint for his birth certificate.

This is the actual footprint of the baby on page 77. See how tiny it is compared with your own!

Short as is mother's stay in the hospital, it is full of business, for whether she has a private room or shares a ward with others, she has a younger baby to care for when she leaves than when she remained two weeks, and must need know more about him. Teaching nurses hold classes for departing mothers concerning the care and feeding of their new babies. They recommend books of established authors and in many cases give the mothers a little handbook of ready reference to take home with them. The private-room mother has the advantage over the others, of course, for she begins at once the personal care of her baby while still under the watchful, skillful guidance of her hospital nurses. Father, too, profits by the system and gets his hand in before he starts off helping on the homework.

Fine as the rooming in system is, it is not new. Before there were maternity hospitals and even afterwards, women made their plans to have their babies born at home. They liked to remain in the midst of their familiar surroundings and, of course, in earlier days it was necessary. A doctor and experienced baby nurse were engaged and grandmother often came from afar to take charge of the household—much to everyone's joy, especially grandmother's, who liked to find herself again at her old familiar task of home and baby tending.

Sometimes, mothers who stay at home find themselves in a predicament. The baby surprises them and

starts to come before he was expected. (It can also
happen to hospital-bound mothers.) Then the city
emergency center gets a call, somebody comes racing
—often a policeman in his truck which is filled with all
the necessary equipment. How many grateful mothers
and fathers there must be who have named their
babies for Johnny-on-the-spot policemen who arrived
in the nick of time!

In foreign countries and in the rural parts of this
country where there are more babies and less money
to pay hospitals and doctors, trained women called
midwives (another funny name) are the substitute.
They make up a large and respected profession who
are required to have special training and a license to
practice the delivery of babies and the aftercare of
them and their mothers. Yes, they are an ancient and
respected institution, active even in Bible times.

Yet everyone needs the modern hospital with all its
up-to-the-minute emergency equipment. If a baby's
little lungs are by chance filled with fluid, they can be
emptied with the exhalator (exhale: to breathe out).
Its action is the opposite of the inhalator (inhale: to
breathe in), which, you remember, we spoke of earlier
as a small oxygen hand pump which doctors use today
to start the breathing of newborn babies when they are
a bit slow in taking over.

But whether the baby arrives in the hospital or at
home, the mother is required to rest in bed for about

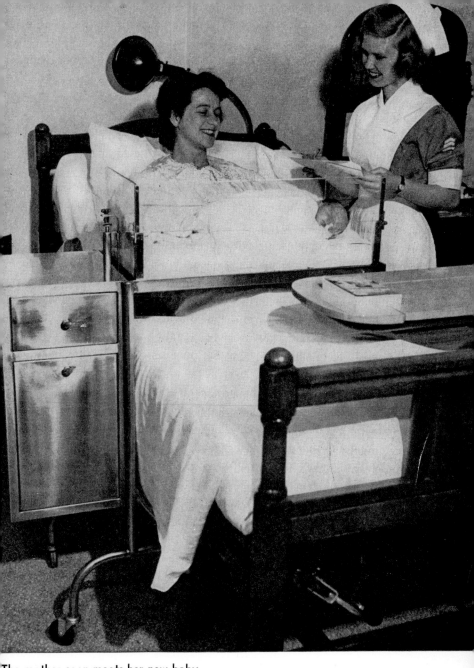

The mother soon meets her new baby.

two weeks. She is not ill, but the parts of her system that sheltered the baby and brought him into the world must be given time to return to their normal everyday condition. Even for several weeks she must be careful not to become overtired.

No doubt some of the following questions have already occurred to you:

1. What happens if a baby isn't born in nine months?

Most babies come along about the time they are expected—sometimes a few days earlier, and sometimes a few days later. But if one should be too long delayed, the doctor in charge would take measures to start the baby on his way. He knows how. He often gives a medicine that starts the contractions of the muscles.

2. How does the mother know when it is time to go to the hospital?

There are several ways of knowing. When the baby is ready to be born, the muscles of the uterus begin to contract and cause pains. These first pains are rather far apart, so that the mother has time to pack her bag and get ready to go. Sometimes the baby's coverings burst and the fluid drains away before the muscles have begun to contract. In either case she has the signal that the baby is on his way.

3. How can animals do without a doctor if human beings can't?

Animals are more rugged. In their natural life in the fields and forests they build up endurance for all kinds of things—for the birth of their young among others. Soon after their babies are born, they are ready to go forth again in search of food. Among primitive peoples, like many tribes in Africa and elsewhere, human mothers were and still are much the same. They work in the fields, come home and deliver their babies, and soon return to their toil carrying their babies on their backs. Civilization has changed matters with its warmer houses, different eating and sleeping habits, slight amounts of exercise. Civilized people are less rugged, more sensitive. They need help. Even animals that have lived among people—house pets and others—are becoming like human beings in their needs for nursing and good care.

4. What is meant by "taking a baby"?

Sometimes a mother is very ill or in such a condition that it does not seem wise for her sake and the sake of the baby to wait until the full term of nine months is passed. In such a situation the doctor brings about the birth of the baby by methods which in many cases are used without harm either to the mother or to the baby.

5. Why are some babies so red when they are born?

A new baby has a very delicate thin skin which allows the color of the blood to show through more plainly than ours does. More than that, the blood of a newborn baby is richer than it is later; it has not yet become thinned out to the color that we are accustomed to see.

6. Why does the baby's skin peel off?

A baby does not perspire for the first month of his life, and the skin is often scaly. If he is cleansed with oil instead of with water, the peeling or scaling is lessened.

7. Can a baby think when he is born? Does he have a mind?

A baby has a brain, a nervous system, and sense organs
—eyes, ears, nose, tongue—which form the equipment that
will develop a mind as he comes more and more in touch
with things and people about him. At birth a baby can
tell light from darkness, but at first his two eyes have not
yet learned to focus well, so objects are a bit blurred. He
can taste with his tongue and cheeks; he can tell hot from
cold; he can feel pain and pressure; and a day or two after
birth he can hear sounds about him. Because little babies
are more sensitive than we are, they must be shielded
from all extremes.

CHAPTER 9

The milk supply

AFTER a baby is born and the old food supply from the mother by way of the placenta has been cut off, little son or daughter is faced with a new situation.

Getting your food in a nice, digested, fluid form delivered straight into your blood, without ever your feeling or knowing anything about it, is one thing; and having to suck it from your mother's breast with your new mouth is quite another. But Nature has no idea of letting her babies starve. Every baby knows how to suck when he is born. His mouth, tongue, and cheeks are all provided with a group of little muscles ready to act.

Just to let a young baby show you how well he knows how to suck, lightly touch his cheek near his mouth with your finger. I hope it is a clean, well-scrubbed, germless finger, because he will turn his head very quickly, and if you don't watch out, he will draw that old, dry finger right into his mouth. If he

Polar bear cubs taking milk from their mother.

does, you'll be surprised at the strength of his pull.
You think he is such a wee, helpless mite. He is, until
food comes his way; then he turns into a live little
dynamo well equipped to do his share in obtaining his
daily bread. Look how hard he works pumping away
with those strong little jaws of his, and see how con-
tent he is after his meal, his stomach happily filled
with warm milk.

Human babies are mammals, just as are all babies
that are fed with mother's milk after they are born—
dogs, zebras, bears, lions, whales, elephants, seals,
bats, and so on. Their name, *mammal,* tells the story,
because the Latin word *mammae* means "breasts."
Mother's name tells the story, too, when we call her
Mamma, although some people say mammas were
given their name by the babies themselves when they
first began to make sounds: "Ma-ma."

All during the period that a baby mammal, either
human or animal, has been growing in its mother, her
breasts have been getting ready to make a plentiful
supply of milk for his first few weeks or months of life.
Inside the breast is a network of tiny tubes leading into
fifteen or twenty larger tubes which open straight into
a mouthpiece on the outside called the *nipple.* Human
mothers have two breasts, just as they have two
ovaries, two eyes, two ears. in accordance with their
twofold plan of structure.

A cow's milk glands are enclosed in one large sac
called an *udder,* which has four *teats* or nipples. Ani-

mal mothers usually have many nipples in two rows
like buttons on a double-breasted coat. The number
depends upon the number of young—cubs, kittens, or
puppies—they usually have. A dog has eight nipples or
teats because her litter numbers usually from six to
eight.

Frequently, there are more, ten or twelve puppies.
The world record, I understand, of dog litters was
twenty-three puppies! This mother had to have two or
three dog wet nurses to help her supply sufficient milk
to feed her oversized family. Wet nurses, human or
animal, supply mother's milk for babies who are not
their own.

Because human milk is the best possible food for
human babies, many women who have more milk than
they need sell it to hospitals. Originally a wet nurse
fed other people's babies at the breast just as she did
her own. Today her milk is frequently expressed by a
breast pump and shipped in proper containers to some
hospital where, together with the milk of other wet
nurses, it is made ready for those babies who require
it.

A few mothers are not able to provide their babies
with mother's milk. They are not well, or their milk is
not suitable. In those instances the babies are given
cow's milk weakened or modified with boiled water.
Such babies are often spoken of as "bottle-fed babies."
With care they may be as sturdy as babies fed on

mother's milk, although mother's milk is usually better and safer.

Some commercial agencies scientifically prepare special milk formulas for the needs of bottle babies. In fact, not only bottles but nipples and nipple protectors —everything is supplied and guaranteed germ proof. What a saving for the busy mother! She has only to bring the formula to the proper temperature and there you are! But, we hope, with all this time saved, it will be set aside to give her the pleasure of holding the baby while he takes his bottle, snugly nestled in her arms. That is much more important than formula filling and no bottle holders can take her place.

The only "bottle holders" that can take her place are little brother or sister, such as the one in the picture on the next page. They seem to be having a beautiful time. Babies like their big brothers and sisters who seem to be especially akin to them; they find their bottle when they lose it (lots of things can happen to bottles when alone), play with them when they are exercising on the floor pad, keep them dry when they are wet, covered when they are cold—all of dozens of nice, comfortable things brothers and sisters can do for the new baby. They all make for friendship when in a few years everybody is grown up, and neither one is "big" or "little"—both are just family and belong to each other.

As a baby grows older, orange juice, strained cereals,

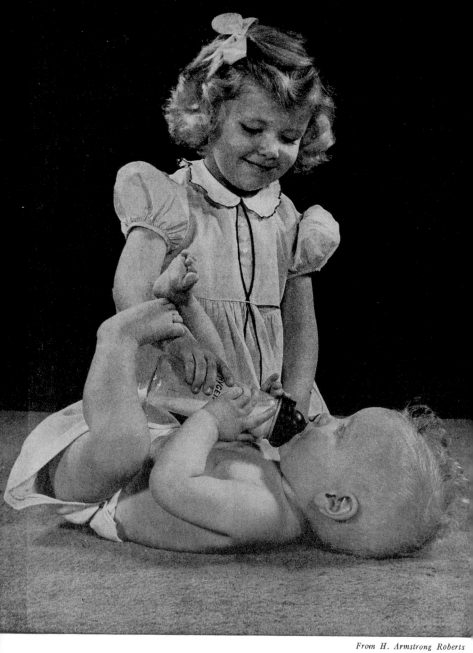

From H. Armstrong Roberts

A little girl giving her new baby brother his bottle.

and other soft foods are added to his diet, so that gradually he is prepared to give up mother's milk for hardier fare.

Of course, in order to have breast milk, all mothers, both human and animal, must have new babies of their own, since only at that time do the milk glands secrete. Breast milk is not just milk that the mother drinks transferred to her breasts. It is made from all the food that she eats. Yet there are certain foods, among them cow's milk, which are known to help generously the quality and quantity of human milk. But all food, including the milk that one drinks, undergoes many changes before it can be used by the body.

Foster mothers

Milk differs in the various animals. It contains the particular food substance that each kind needs for its growth. Cows, goats, and reindeer are good milk producers. People up in the icy lands raise their herds of milk reindeer just as we raise our herds of Jersey or Holstein cows. Goat's milk is very like human milk and is easily digested. Many a milk-filled nanny has saved the life of a little newborn baby when his mother could not feed him herself. Animals, like human beings, often serve as foster mothers or wet nurses to other animals. A calf whose mother has very desirable milk for the market is frequently fed by another cow whose milk is less salable. Sometimes the baby calf's wet nurse is just a tin pail. Then he has to be taught to drink. The dairyman holds the baby nose down close to the milk so that the calf can smell it. Then he puts his finger dipped in milk into the calf's mouth to start the sucking movements. In a few minutes the milk is taken by the calf without the helping finger.

Mother dogs are very hospitable to stray puppies and even to stray kittens. They often serve as foster mothers to lion cubs in a zoölogical park, for now and then a lion mother in captivity will refuse to feed her babies. Elephant mothers, too, will give a neighbor baby a drink of milk if his mother is not at hand. Some animals are not so kind, and a seal baby that tries to steal a swallow from a strange mother seal is likely to find himself tossed into mid-air like an old shoe.

Somehow or other, all these nursing mothers make you feel that there is a real kinship between them. From the tiny monkey nursing her wispy baby in her arms, or the big, fat, blobby seal with her flippers affectionately encircling the slippery body of the baby seal, up to the human mother, you see the same loyalty and devotion. It is all one, and it goes by the name of mother love.

And now for some final questions that are often asked:

I. Where does the milk come from?

It is made right in the mother's breasts just for the baby. Only mothers of new babies have milk. When a cow has milk, it is because she is the mother of a new baby calf.

We take part of the cow's milk, and the farmer lets the calves have the rest, or he separates the cream and lets the calves have the skimmed milk that remains.

2. Why can't Father feed the baby?

Fathers have no milk. Only mothers have milk for their babies. They shelter and nourish the babies before they are born and continue to nourish them for a short time afterward. A father does his part, as we know, in helping start the baby and afterward by providing a home for his family and giving them his love and care.

3. But Father has nipples. Why are they there?

At the very beginning, before they are born, all babies are made very much the same. If you could see a baby embryo, you wouldn't be able to tell whether it was going to be a little boy or a little girl. The sex organs are very much alike at first. If the baby is to be a girl, the parts that could have made a boy do not develop. If the baby is to be a boy, the parts that would have made a girl do not develop. The breasts are just one of the parts that do not develop further in boys because they will not need them.

4. What is meant by weaning a baby?

Weaning is the term used for changing a baby's diet from breast milk to bottle or cow's milk. The weaning takes place gradually over a period of weeks, so that the baby may become accustomed to the new method of feed-ing and not be disturbed by it.

CHAPTER 10

Twins and multiple births

EVER since back in the 1930's when five little girls, the Dionnes, were born to one mother at the same time, multiple births (many at a time) seem to have become the fashion. It is probably because we hear more about them today, for one thing, and more of them live to grow up.

The words *quintuplets, quadruplets,* and their like are interesting and not so difficult as they seem. They are just variations of an old familiar word, *duplicate*—to make twice alike, or two of a kind. We don't say, "He is a duplicate," but we could. We use instead the word *twin,* a form of the old Saxon word *twain,* meaning two. It is the same word *Mark Twain* took for his pen name. *Triplets* is easily seen to be a shortened form of triplicate, three of a kind; and then we say *quadruplets,* four of a kind, *quintuplets,* five of a kind, *sextuplets,* six of a kind, *septuplets,* seven of a kind, and so on, except when the newspapers shorten them down to "quints" and "quads" in true American fashion.

Twins

To begin at the beginning, there are two kinds of twins, known as *unlike twins* and *identical twins.* Almost every school has an example of both kinds.

Unlike twins, also called *fraternal twins,* are just two children who happen to be born of the same mother at the same time. They may be two brothers, two sisters, or a brother and sister. Though often they look alike, they may be quite different from each other—one tall, the other short; one dark, the other light; one a curly-head, the other straight-haired, just as any two chil-

Unlike twins form in separate sacs and are nourished by two placentae.

Courtesy of Maternity Center Association

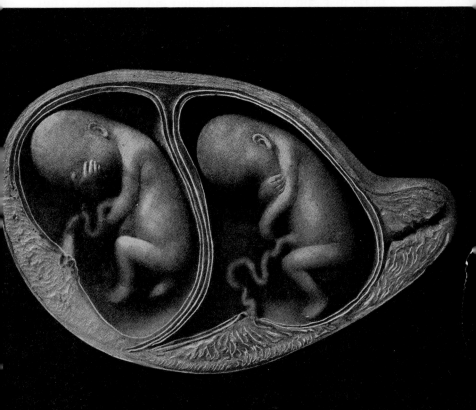

dren in the same family may differ who are born years apart.

These unlike twins are often called "two-egg twins." Two egg cells have broken away from the ovary at the same time; both have traveled down the Fallopian tube, and because more than one sperm cell was present, both were fertilized. These twins, one may believe, are the result of two separate egg cells fertilized by two sperm cells. They are called twins merely because they were born at the same time.

Identical twins

Identical twins are real twins. They were intended to be just one person and turned out to be two. They

A healthy pair of identical twins.

From H. Armstrong Roberts

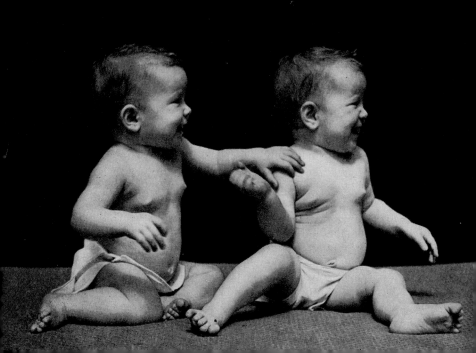

are always of the same sex—either two boys or two girls. No opposites in identical twins. They are duplicates in earnest. They are often so much alike that their own mother cannot tell them apart. As for their teacher, she never knows which is which. Either may be reciting. Being an identical twin has its advantages.

How are they made? They are the result of a split in the early stages of cell division. You remember how the fertilized cell divides into two:

Suppose each one of these turned its back on the other, so to speak, and instead of going on to make the single embryo that it started out to make, each half went on by itself and made a complete embryo on its own hook.

You'd think that each half would turn out just half a baby. No, in these first divisions, cells are not ready to make organs or parts of the body. They just make cells and more cells. If you watch an earthworm that has been cut in the middle, you can see how this happens. In no time at all the tail end will grow a head, and the head end will grow a tail. The earthworm is an example of the ability of cells to produce a whole from a part. Its cells' substance is not highly specialized. In the early stages of the human embryo the cells are not highly specialized either. They are like the earthworm in this respect.

Triplets and quadruplets

If you can, imagine the original fertilized cell dividing a second time like this:

and each of the four cells going on independently to produce its own embryo—sphere, mulberry, layers of cells, everything complete—then you can see how *quadruplets* could be accounted for. If two of the four went on independently and each developed an embryo while two remained together and made just one embryo, *triplets* might result—one-egg triplets:

Quintuplets and *sextuplets* would require one more division. Suppose we say that three of the four cells went on and each made its little embryo by dividing and multiplying as usual. Suppose the fourth cell divided and the separated halves stayed separate and each made an embryo of its own. That would make two more embryos. Three and two make five. There are your quintuplets. You can easily see how sextuplets would result if another of the cells did the same thing. If *all* of the eight cells of the third division remained independent of each other and each one developed an embryo, you would have eight embryos. But that wonder has never been recorded, I think, except by hearsay.

Triplets, quadruplets, and quintuplets are not necessarily formed from one fertilized cell. They may result from one, two, three, four—any one of a series of combinations. One single child and a pair of twins would make triplets, for example. Two single children and a pair of twins would make quadruplets. Two pairs of twins would also make quadruplets. The combinations are many, and in these instances the children are not all identical. Many of them belong to the class of unlike twins.

The well-known quintuplets in South America are not like the Dionne quints—all identicals. The South American children are two boys and three girls, which means, as we know, the results of at least two different fertilizations, since identicals must all be of the same sex.

These are theories that scientists offer to account for identical twins and multiple births. No one has actually seen human twins formed from these early cell divisions, but such an explanation seems reasonable and coincides with what is known of cell habits in general.

Siamese twins

Siamese twins are nearer by one step to the original single person that they were really intended to be.

They failed to separate completely. The cell mass held at just one point like this:

Sometimes the point of union in the resulting twins turns out to be in the middle of the back, sometimes in the middle of the front, sometimes at the sides. It is like an isthmus of land between two continents.

We used to wonder how Siamese twins could sit down and move about with any degree of comfort and freedom. In most cases, the stretch of tissue is not rigid like the bar of a dumbbell in the gymnasium. It is flexible, bends and allows the twins to turn and bend, too. But so long as the bar held, they were captive and couldn't get away from each other. With Stevenson they could only say, "I have a little shadow that goes in and out with me." But which was the shadow? That was the question. There must have been some stiff disagreements on many points. However, today, in this wonderful age of progress in matters technical, including the science of medicine and surgery, the end of Siamese imprisonment seems at hand.

Litters

Animals that usually have single babies, such as the cow or horse, sometimes have twins just as human mothers have. But animals that have many young at a time, such as the dog, the cat, the rabbit, the pig, and others, have *litters*. Even if there were just two babies, it would be a litter of two, not twins, usually. Twins in these animals are very rare.

In litters of puppies, let us say, each puppy has its own placenta and its own protective coat and cord. They are brother and sister puppies, and each comes from the fertilization of a single egg cell by a single sperm cell. The puppies may be quite different in their markings—spotted or all white or all black—according to their breed. They correspond to unlike twins in human beings.

It is always possible to know at birth whether babies are identical or unlike twins. Identical twins always develop from one placenta and share a single outer protective covering. Unlike twins usually develop from two placentas, but in any case each has its own separate outer sac. Multiple babies, whether in twos or threes or fours or whatever their number, are normal human beings. They are entitled to live normal human lives, to go to school and play and have friends like other children. Science is making these children strong and well. The public must help make them happy.

Incubators

Most babies who are born many at a time come a bit earlier than single babies. Such births are called *premature*. The more babies there are, the more likely they are to be pushed out ahead of time. They crowd each other, and they crowd the uterus so that it gets impatient and begins the churnings and pressings that send the little passengers on their way. Single babies at times are prematurely born, too, for various reasons. Because they are not fully matured or developed, these tiny babies often weigh but a pound or two each.

Such early-born babies must be tucked away quickly into a warm and cozy incubator if they are to live. An incubator is a device for saving babies that are born too soon. It is a case or box or even a baby's crib which is fitted up in such a way that in it are provided the same conditions that a baby would have had if he had remained in his mother, so that there is the same temperature, the same degree of moisture, the same amount of oxygen. Every detail is carefully reproduced. The little scrap of a premature baby is wrapped at first in cotton wool or some other soft and delicate substance, fed mother's milk or perhaps, for a time, just sugar and water; and he is so comfortable and contented that he doesn't miss his abandoned place inside of his mother.

Incubators today are growing better and better like iron lungs and saving thousands of babies that might otherwise not have lived—twins, multiple babies who crowd each other out too soon, and, of course, little Siamese babies who are struggling to recover themselves from the surgery undertaken to separate them.

Nature has provided some of her animals with natural incubators. Kangaroo mothers have a pouch or pocket in their coats in which the baby kangaroos hang up by their mouths on her teats or nipples like soft little garments on closet hooks. At mealtime, the pegs supply warm milk.

Most of you can understand baby incubators because you have seen a chicken incubator. In a square box or case fitted with warm coils of pipes heated by lamps or electricity, hundreds of eggs can be hatched out at a time. Some incubators have a device for turning the eggs over just as the mother hen would do in order that they might be warmed on all sides. The sad part of the story is that baby chicks hatched out in incubators have no nice clucking mother to go about with them and spread her wings for them when it rains or danger threatens. The poultry man usually has a brooder, a tent-shaped cover with a large lamp beneath, under which hundreds of little cheepers may snuggle, but it could never be mistaken for sheltering mother wings.

Anyway, if incubators are not quite the same as mothers, they have saved some very valuable little people to this world of ours.

From *H. Armstrong Roberts*

A father playing with his baby daughter.

CHAPTER 11

Like father, like son

WHAT sort of person is a certain baby to be? Will he have curly hair or straight? Will he be tall or short? Will he have a full, deep chest or a shallow, narrow one?

You may recall that we mentioned back in Chapter 2 that the reproductive cells hold the pattern or design for each new person that is to be built. The pattern in each of the two reproductive cells, egg and sperm, is found in a little string of beadlike bodies called *chromosomes*. In these groups of chromosomes are hidden away the pattern of the various traits or characteristics of each parent—long fingers or short, blue eyes or brown, light complexion or dark, small feet or large, straight nose or arched. All sorts of traits, usually quite different from one another, are packed away in the two sets of chromosomes.

You'd think Nature would be in a great quandary and not know what to do when in her fertilized cell she found two sets of patterns for one individual baby.

Which set should she use? You would not think it fair
to make him entirely like father or entirely like mother.
No more does Nature. Instead, very carefully she takes
part of the sperm chromosomes and part of the egg
chromosomes and mixes them up together. Out comes,
as you have guessed, not an exact copy of father nor
an exact copy of mother, but a new pattern which is
like neither and yet is like both, because it is a com-
bination of the two.

Sometimes in the shake-up a better array of traits is
gathered together than those present in either father
or mother, and rather plain-looking parents produce a
beautiful child. At other times the shake-up brings a
poor lot of traits together, and very good-looking parents produce an ugly duckling. But the ugly ducklings
mustn't be discouraged. Features—chin, nose, mouth,
jaw—change with the years, so that unbeautiful children often become very fine-looking men and women.

Sometimes we find a trait in ourselves that is lacking
in both father and mother. It seems to have sprung out
of nowhere. Perhaps it is a liking for roving about and
finding new places. Mother doesn't account for it. She
doesn't care to rove. Father doesn't account for it. He
sits all day. But just let grandmother arrive. She will
explain it. "You say that boy won't stay put? Of course
not. Look at his grandfather, before the mast when
he was seventeen."

Whether you inherited the roving spirit from grandfather or not, one does inherit not only from parents,

but also from grandparents, great-grandparents and great-great-grandparents, and so on back.

You have heard people say that a person comes from "good old stock." When we come from good old stock, good things are expected of us. There is another expression: "Blood will tell." It means the same thing. Besides the physical qualities that our parents pass on to us, we inherit also mental traits, qualities of mind. We are quick at figures or the opposite—we hate arithmetic. We are musical or we have no ear. We are born mechanics or we can't strike a nail on the head. All kinds of talents—art, music, writing—run in families, although, of course, they must be developed and improved by study and hard work. One can remain unaware of a talent such as music because no attempt has been made to develop it. On the other hand, study and hard work may do a great deal to develop an art when little inherited talent exists. One thing is sure: our ancestors cannot pass on to us anything that was not theirs to pass along. You can't give what you never owned.

Two boys sat in the same room at school. One was named Antonio. He was a short, stocky fellow with a rich deep-olive skin and fine dark eyes. The other boy was Olaf. Olaf was tall and blond and broad-shouldered. Antonio would look across the room at Olaf and wish he could grow up to be tall and blond and broad-shouldered. Then nobody would call him "Dagie." Olaf would look across the room at Antonio and wish he could be dark and handsome and heavy-set; then nobody would call him "Whitie." These wishes could never come true, for tall people and light-haired people had not contributed to the pattern of Antonio's making, and short, stocky people with dark hair and eyes had not contributed to the pattern of Olaf's making.

A great many things that people think are inherited are not inherited at all. If a person has only three fingers on one hand because he lost two by accident, there is no reason to think that his children's hands will have but three fingers. Even if a person had but three fingers when he was born, his children need not necessarily have but three fingers. The defect may have been caused by some difficulty which arose at the time he was being formed. If the embryo had not been properly attached so that the placenta could do its work of building up the body adequately; if the mother were suffering from certain diseases that could affect the normal development of the cells; if the temperature within the uterus were lowered and the supply of oxygen interfered with for any reason, then the baby could suffer a faulty growth—fingers or toes or other parts might not be perfectly formed. Defects of this nature are called *congenital* defects. They are present at birth. When they arise from such accidental causes, they are not passed on from parents to child. Congenital defects are fairly frequent, but they are found in only a relatively small number of babies born.

Think of how few people you know who are crippled or blind or deaf at birth. Most of us are fairly good examples of Nature's skill. If anyone we know has a defect, the courteous thing to do is to disregard it.

Birthmarks

Birthmarks, those patches of red, purple, or brown which one sees on peoples' faces or necks or arms, are familiar to all of us, and we wonder what caused them. The red ones are due to an enlargement of tiny blood vessels that got in a jam and didn't develop quite properly. The brown ones are due to some defect in the pigment or coloring matter of the body. In both cases something went wrong in Nature's loom. Birthmarks are like the rough, uneven places in cloth where in the weaving the threads got thickened and tangled in one spot.

You may hear someone say that a birthmark is caused by something that frightened the person's mother while, as a baby, he was growing in her. If the patch is red, she is assumed to have been frightened by a burning house or to have suffered from a desire for cherries or some other red fruit. If the patch is brown, then the mother is said to have been frightened by a mouse or rabbit or some other brown animal that ran across her path. Silly old tales!

If you ask when the house burned or the rabbit jumped, you'll be told, "Oh, just a month before the baby was born." Now you know and I know that the baby's skin, his blood vessels, and the coloring matter are formed long before a month of his birth. Any spots of that sort would have had to be built in at the very outset of embryonic life, when the three layers of cells first began to do their special work.

There are a few illnesses and diseases which could harm the baby with their germs. If the mother were very, very ill with typhoid fever or influenza, the embryo might be affected, and perhaps it might be injured in some other way. But in general it is not an easy matter for a baby in the making to be affected by anything that happens to his mother. He is too well protected by his wrappings and by the placenta, which filters out impure substances from his mother's blood On the whole, Nature takes very good care of her babies and does not leave many chances open for injury to happen to them.

Mixed matings

To return to our topic of inheritance, very few characteristics or traits are passed on without modification or change. We can't put our finger on anything and say, "I inherited this from my father." Those traits which are passed on are subject to certain laws. Take a basket of puppies, for instance. You have all seen them, round little balls of fur with straight-out tails and sprawly little legs. Brothers and sisters, yet with so many different markings that you might think the mother dog had adopted them or collected them one by one around the neighborhood.

There was Curly, a dark reddish spaniel. One day she presented her master with four puppies, two like herself, one black, and one a beautiful golden red. Duke, the father, was a spaniel, darkish red, too, like Curly. Wouldn't you have thought that all the puppies would have been like their parents? Where did the black one come from, and where did they get the

ixed mating results in hybrids.

is chart illustrates xed mating in which e trait does not com- etely hide another but ows itself as a cross tween the two.

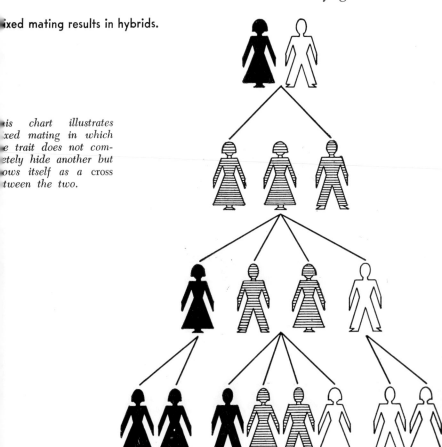

golden one? I'll tell you. There is a ghost in Curly's and Duke's closet. They are not "pure-bred"! They are *hybrids* or *crossbreeds*—sometimes called *mongrels*. Somewhere along the line there had been some cross-mating, that is, matings between two breeds. If you had looked into the matter, you would have found that both Duke and Curly were each the result of a mating between a black spaniel and a golden spaniel. Now you see where the odd puppies came from—black from the black spaniel grandparents, golden from the golden

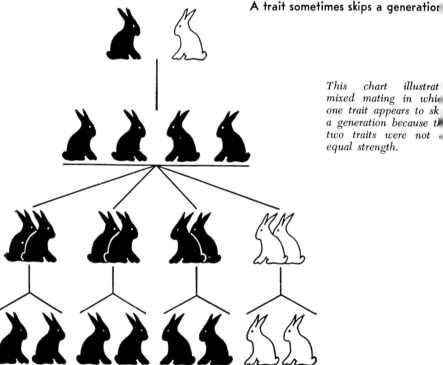

A trait sometimes skips a generation

This chart illustrat mixed mating in whic one trait appears to sk a generation because t two traits were not equal strength.

grandparents. The other two, the dark reddish ones, were hybrids like the parents, Duke and Curly.

The next generation will surprise you. If there are no more cross-matings—that is, if, when the puppies grow up, they mate only with their own kind—the black spaniels will always have black puppies and the golden spaniels will have golden puppies. None of them will look at all like the grandparents, Duke and Curly. Whichever way the mixed puppies mate, some of their puppies will be mixed, too, but if they keep on breeding "pure," the time will come when there will be no more traces of the mixture.

The story is not always so simple. Sometimes we are mixtures or crossbreeds in regard to this or that trait, and we don't show it. The traits that we inherit are not of equal strength. If mother has blue eyes, for example, and father has brown, the blue are likely to get pushed aside to a great extent. If there are four children, three of them will have brown eyes, and just one will have blue. But don't think that the blue is lost in all the brown-eyed children. It's hiding in two of them. They carry the trait and will pass both blue eyes and brown eyes on to their children. The third brown-eyed one is "pure" and will pass on brown eyes, just as the blue-eyed one will pass on blue eyes to the next generation. Most people illustrate this law of the unequal strength of traits in one or more of their characteristics. We say that a certain trait "skips" a generation. It appears in a parent, disappears in his child, and reappears in his grandchild.

Mixtures of race

In our country we are familiar with the children of
mixed marriages. In many schools today there are
boys and girls who are children of the union between
a Negro and a white parent. They are called *mulattos.*
If the parents are mulattos and just one of the four
grandparents is a Negro, then the grandchildren are
called *quadroons,* which means they have one-fourth
Negro blood. If only one of the eight great-grandparents was a Negro, then the children are called *octo-
roons,* which means they have but one-eighth Negro
blood. If there were no more marriages with Negroes,
in time the dark color would disappear and be "bred
out." Usually mulattos marry other mulattos, so the
mixture continues. After several generations of such
marriages it would be difficult to say just what color
the children would be. In one family of seven children,
one was so light he could have passed for white, one
was so black he looked like a full-blooded Negro, while
the other five were dark brown in the case of three
and light brown in the case of two. Yet they were
brothers and sisters, children of mulatto parents.

So-called mixed marriages, that is—marriage between different kinds of people (in race, religion, even
nationality)—are becoming more and more usual. Buy-
ing and selling among each other's countries, studying
in the same schools, defending each other's countries,

all bring people closer together. They learn to like and respect each other.

Not long ago, people thought that children of mixed marriages suffered because they felt "neither one thing or the other" among their playmates. They felt they didn't belong. Often they didn't, unfortunately. The correction for that feeling is for everybody to accept everyone else so far as "race, color and creed" is concerned. Then each one will belong. He will make his place in the world by what he is himself. Such acceptance of each other does not come suddenly. It comes gradually, little by little, as people work and play together, friends and fellow students at school. We only hope our American way of life will become as acceptable to others as their own way was to them in the beginning. Each one loves his own, his native land, and it is hard to change.

Marriage between cousins

Marriage between cousins is not a union of unlikes, but a union of likes. "Never marry your cousin," people say, "or your children will be defective." What about it? Will they be? That depends. You remember that you cannot inherit what isn't first possessed to transmit. If two cousins, or people otherwise closely related, could be found who came from a family in which there were no weaknesses, there could be no weaknesses passed on to their children. But if there were a defect, such as a tendency to insanity in the family, there would be a greater chance of passing it on if both father and mother came from the same family. It would be just as undesirable to marry a person who was not your cousin if that person had the same defects in his family that yours had. It isn't being cousins or closely related that matters, it is the danger of multiplying defects that are likely to be carried on to the children. Anyway, this is a good thing to remember: we are all chips off the old block, and that is all right if the block comes from a fine sound tree.

A mother swan leading her family. The father, bringing up the rear, makes certain everything goes smoothly.

CHAPTER 12

Mating and marrying

From our talk on
patterns, personal traits, and heredity you could easily
begin to think that there was little left for each person
to do about himself. It looked as though Nature had
just cut us out with a family cookie cutter, each cookie
having a little more or a little less brown or a little
larger or smaller scallop.

You were not intended to look at it quite that way.
Human beings are not like their animal cousins. Because they have been made on a rather simpler plan
than humans, Nature has given animals more definite
rules of what to do and how and when to do it. She not
only has made a framework, but she has contrived to
install some self-running machinery in it. The self-
running machinery is called *instinct*.

If, for instance, you were a kind of solitary wasp,
you'd know without being taught the particular kind
of spider you should hunt for your new baby's food.
After you had caught the spider and killed or paralyzed

it, you would wall it up with one of your wasp eggs. When the baby hatched out, there would be his spider meal in the icebox. Insects, birds, and animals with the littlest minds follow their instinct patterns exactly. They do not change them. Higher animals have a mixture of both instinct and intelligence. They can learn to do things and learn not to do things, so that they can change their patterns once in a while. Sometimes animals seem to have almost human intelligence. How often we hear of a dog rescuing his master from threatening danger. How intelligent must be those German police dogs that are being trained to guide the blind through the city streets! As the mind develops, the instinct machinery runs down. It is partly run down in the higher animals. It is almost completely run down in human beings. Nature has given over to us the job of running ourselves and expects us to apply our intelligence to the task.

Human beings and their animal cousins have much in common. They both must seek food and shelter, escape from danger, find mates, produce their babies, and care for them. But the ways they go about these things are vastly different.

Think of the way an animal satisfies his hunger. If, for example, he is a lion, he stalks his prey, kills it, tears it apart, and eats it greedily with a snap and a growl at anyone else that seeks to interfere.

People make a social occasion of eating. They sit down together, father, mother, and children. There is a lace or linen cloth on the table, pretty china, bright silver and glass, flowers. Everyone talks and laughs, tells the events of the day, and enjoys the good warm food. Most of us do not realize how important a part of eating the company, the flowers, and all the prettinesses are until we do without them. Sit down alone and try to eat your dinner on a newspaper with an iron spoon from an iron pot, and see what would happen to your appetite. It would leave you. You'd say, "I'm not hungry. I don't want any dinner." We have become social, beauty-loving creatures. We have progressed far beyond the jungle.

The same thing is true of the other hunger, mate hunger. Human mating has become just as different from the mating of animals as our mealtimes have become different from theirs. The decorations of mating—love-making—are not practiced by animals to any extent. They are not very choosy. Mate-getting is rather a matter of convenience. Many animals have special periods of mating and follow a fixed routine. Once or twice a year they are ready to mate. At such periods they are said to be "in heat" or "rut," and they send out mating signals to each other. A female dog, for instance, gives off a special odor which attracts the male dog to her. If she is not ready to mate, there is no odor to carry her message. Male and female animals that are not in heat would not be attracted toward each other. No male would think of approaching a female that was not ready. This is the law of the animal world. After mating has taken place, the mother is left by herself to await her young and care for them when they are born.

Animals mate only with their own kind—dogs with dogs, cats with cats, sheep with sheep, and horses with horses. A dog will mate with another kind of dog—a collie with a setter, for example—but never with a cat. Some of us used to think that dogs were fathers and we called them all "he," and that cats were mothers and we called them all "she," but we never saw any babies that were half dog and half cat.

The monkey tribe does not have seasons of mating. Monkeys are like human beings in their mating habits. They are ready at any time when they wish to mate. A monkey chooses his wife, courts her, wins her, marries her, and brings up his family in almost human fashion.

Like birds, many monkeys attract their mates by their bright colors. Most of us who visit the zoölogical parks have noticed the bright red, blue, orange, and green patches of bare skin on their rear ends and on their faces. Some monkeys have funny spreading ruffs and whiskers about their faces that make them look like somebody's old uncle. When the monkeys wish to attract or go courting, they turn around and show off their bright patches. To us this display seems a bit immodest, considering where the colored areas are. We have been taught to keep our bodies covered before others, especially the rear end or buttocks.

In modesty lies one of the great differences between

ANIMAL MATES AND THEIR YOUNG

FAMILY	FATHER	MOTHER	YOUNG
Bear	*He-bear*	*She-bear*	*Cub*
Cat	*Tomcat*	*Queen* [1] *or tabby-cat* [2]	*Kitten*
Cattle	*Bull*	*Cow*	*Calf*
Deer	*Stag or buck*	*Doe*	*Fawn*
Dog	*Dog*	*Bitch*	*Puppy*
Ducks	*Drake*	*Duck*	*Duckling*
Fowl	*Cock or rooster*	*Hen*	*Chick*
Geese	*Gander*	*Goose*	*Gosling*
Goat	*Buck or billy-goat* [2]	*Doe or nanny-goat* [2]	*Kid*
Horse	*Stallion*	*Mare*	*Colt*
Lion	*Lion*	*Lioness*	*Cub*
Mule (hybrid)	*Donkey*	*Mare*	*Colt*
Pigeon	*Cock*	*Hen*	*Squab*
Rabbit	*Buck*	*Doe*	*Rabbit or bunny* [2]
Seal	*Bull*	*Cow*	*Pup*
Sheep	*Ram*	*Ewe*	*Lamb*
Swine	*Boar*	*Sow*	*Pig or shote*

[1] Especially of fancy breeds.
[2] Popular usage.

ourselves and our animal cousins. Keeping sheltered from others those parts of us which are concerned with mating and with the disposal of bodily wastes is a mark of our higher social development. It is the distinction of human beings. Even among the savage tribes on the islands of the sea where brown bodies are gleaming everywhere, the reproductive or mating organs are usually covered.

Instead of using bodily colors to attract each other, men and women use color in dress, personal decoration and hair arrangements, voice, gesture, words, song, smiles, gifts—all sorts of things. Boys like to use athletic ability—swimming, running, jumping—to attract and please the girls whom they admire. Girls dress in gay colors, dance, sing, laugh, and play, too, in various ways. All of these modes of attraction are Nature's way of helping boys and girls to know and find each other, and they are normal, happy things to do.

When, at thirteen or fourteen, the sperm cells or egg cells begin to awaken, the whole body begins to awaken, too, and change its appearance. Boys grow broader-shouldered and more muscular. Their genital organs (the penis and the testicles) increase in size, their voices become deeper after a period of unevenness which lasts but a short time, and a beard begins to grow upon their faces. For a while they look rather fuzzy and unfinished, but in no time they are so strong and good-looking that all the girls wish for dates.

Girls change, too. They become rounder, in arms, legs, breasts, hips, and because they are rounder they are prettier. Their hair becomes brighter and glossier and their skin clearer. They do not seem at all like the girls the boys used to consider a bother. They seem rather desirable and nice.

Mating time comes eight or ten years later, when school is over, work has begun, and the years between have taught what sort of mate one wishes. Human beings, above all others, should choose their mates with great care. Every boy knows in his heart the sort of girl he thinks he would like to marry. And every girl knows the sort of boy she thinks she would like to marry. You grow up with such a picture in your heart. Then one day, when you are older and ready to marry, the ideal comes to life quite suddenly. Hair, hands, laugh, smiles, may be different from your picture. No matter. It is the ideal just the same, and you love it dearly.

Loving is a part of mating and marriage. It is a warm inner feeling a man and a woman have for each other which makes them sure they belong to each other. When it comes hand in hand with their cherished ideals, their old heart's picture, then they long to draw close together in a personal oneness of mind and body. Most of us cannot think of our fathers and mothers as not belonging to each other. Their life together, caring for each other and for their children, has made them two parts of a whole. Men and women who live in love as husbands and wives and fathers and mothers are held close together by this inner bond. They feel it deeply, and others who know them feel it too.

A modern statue of a young woman by Laura Gardin Fraser.

Unhappily, there are many counterfeits of love and counterfeits of marriage. They need not deceive us. You have seen many a leaden counterfeit quarter or half dollar. You have heard its dull, lifeless thud upon

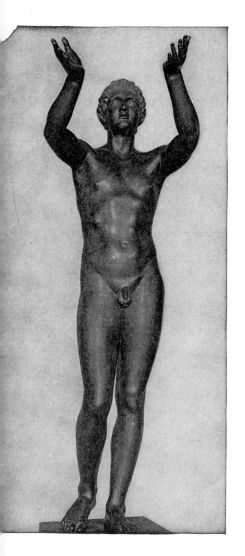

An ancient Greek statue showing the male body.

Courtesy Metropolitan Museum of Art

the counter. Then you have felt the rich smoothness of real coin and heard the true ring of genuine metal. For counterfeit love-making and counterfeit mating there should be no place. There must be no make-believe and love must ring true when fathers and mothers-to-be are choosing each other. Love for one's friends and family is true love, too, but it is so different a kind of love one rarely makes a mistake. If we are to be genuine husbands and wives and love is to ring true when we grow up, we must have no counterfeits along the way. We must save the love acts and the mating acts for the chosen one.

It is wonderful to grow up to live a man's life with all the great things in the world that a man can do. It is wonderful to grow up to live a woman's life with all the great things in the world that a woman can do. Most wonderful of all is the union of two lives, a man's and a woman's, that they may start other lives of new men and women who are to follow and do still greater things.

A list of words and their meanings

Abdomen (*ăb-dō'mĕn*). The part of the body which contains the stomach, intestines, uterus, etc.

Afterbirth. The placenta and protective sacs expelled from the uterus after a baby is born.

Albino (*ăl-bī'no*). A person or animal without bodily coloring matter or pigment.

Albumin (*ăl-bū'mĭn*). The white food substance in the egg.

Alimentary canal (*ăl-ĭ-mĕn'tă-rĭ*). The tube, extending from the mouth to the anus, in which our food is digested.

Anesthetic (*ăn-ĕs-thĕt'ĭk*). Something that deadens the sense of feeling, and also, at times, deprives of consciousness.

Anus (*ā'nŭs*). The opening of the rectum.

Birth. Leaving the mother's body and coming into the world to be a separate individual. The process of being born.

Birth canal. See *Vagina*.

Birthmark. A permanent defect on the surface of the body at birth.

Bladder (*blăd'ĕr*). The sac which holds the urine before it is discharged.

Blood vessels (*vĕs"ls*). The tubes that carry the blood through the body.

Breast. The gland that supplies milk for the new baby.

Brooder. An apparatus for mothering baby chicks.

Buttocks (*bŭt'ŏks*). The rear end. The fatty cushion back of the hips on which one sits.

Cell. A small particle of living matter of which individuals are made.

Chest. The part of the body enclosed by the ribs and breast-bone.

Chromosomes (*krō'mō-sōms*). The small bodies in living cells which carry the inheritance factors, that is, the traits we receive from our parents.

Circumcision (*sir-kŭm-sĭzh'ŭn*). Removal of the foreskin for religious or hygienic reasons.

Coitus (*ko'ĭ-tŭs*). Uniting of husband and wife. The act of human mating.

Congenital (*kŏn-jĕn'ĭ-tăl*). Present at the time of birth.

Copulate (*kŏp'ū-lāt*). To unite so that the sperm cells are transferred from male to female (said of animals chiefly).

Cord. See *Umbilical cord.*

Crossbreed. See *Hybrid.*

Defecate (*dĕf'ē-kāt*). To discharge the solid waste of the alimentary canal through the anus.

Defect. Something which prevents a thing or a person from being perfect.

Delivery. The act of giving birth to young, used, for example, in such phrases as "a normal delivery."

Ectoderm (*ĕk'tō-dŭrm*). The outer of the three germ layers of cells from which the various parts of the body are formed.

Egg cell. An ovum. A tiny particle of living reproductive matter which the mother contributes toward the formation of the new baby, human or animal.

Embryo (*ĕm'brĭ-ō*). Name given to the young during the early stages of development before birth or hatching from the egg.

Endoderm (*ĕn'dō-dŭrm*). The inner of the three germ layers of cells from which the various parts of the body are formed.

Epididymis (*ĕp'ĭ-dĭd'ĭ-mĭs*). A network of tubes connecting the testicle with the vas deferens.

Erection. The state of becoming hard and erect; what occurs in the penis when the bladder is full, or when it is ready for the discharge of the sperm fluid.

Fallopian tubes (*fă-lō′pĭ-ăn*). The passages which carry the egg cells from the ovaries.

Female. The individual that carries the egg cells.

Fertile. Capable of producing offspring.

Fertilization (*fŭr′tĭ-lĭ-zā′shŭn*). The fusion or union of the sperm cell and the egg cell.

Fetus (*fē′tŭs*). Name given the developing individual during the latter part of its growth in the mother.

Fontanelle (*fŏn-tă-něl′*). The soft spot on a baby's head where the bones of the skull have not yet fused.

Foreskin. The loose cap of skin which pulls back from the head of the penis.

Foster mother. One who gives mother care to a child not her own.

Generate (*jěn′ěr-āt*). To produce, as offspring.

Generation (*jěn-ěr-ā′shŭn*). The act of generating; also, people who live at the same time, as "past or future generations."

Generative system (*jěn-ěr-ā′tĭv*). The reproductive system. The organs which produce the sperm and egg cells.

Genes (*jēns*). The individual parts that are thought to make up the chromosomes.

Genital (*jěn′ĭ-tăl*). Belonging to the generative system or reproductive system, as "the genital organs."

Gland. An organ which secretes certain substances, as a tear gland or a sweat gland or a mammary gland.

Heredity (*hě-rěd′ĭ-tĭ*). The passing on of traits from one generation to the next generation.

Hybrid (*hī′brĭd*). An individual resulting from the mating of parents of different variety or species. The mule, offspring of the donkey and the mare, is a hybrid.

Incubator (*ĭn′kū-bā-tĕr*). An apparatus (case or box) for housing babies that are born too early.

Inheritance (*ĭn-hĕr′ĭ-tăns*). That which we receive from our parents and other ancestors.

Instinct (*ĭn′stĭngkt*). A natural inner drive to act in a certain way without being taught.

Intelligence (*ĭn-tĕl′ĭ-jĕns*). Ability to think and understand.

Intercourse. Same as *Coitus*.

Intestines (*ĭn-tĕs′tĭns*). The long tube connecting the stomach with the anus.

Labor. Term used for the pain that arises at childbirth. Labor pains.

Litter. Young that are born at the same time to a parent that usually has many at a time, as the cat, dog, and rabbit.

Male. The individual that carries the sperm cells.

Mammal (*măm′ăl*). An animal that suckles its young, that is, feeds it at the breast with mother's milk.

Mammary gland (*măm′ă-rĭ*). Gland that secretes mother's milk. The breast.

Mates. Husband and wife, or two animals, one male and the other female, in the same relationship.

Mating. The coming together of male and female for the purpose of starting new life.

Menstruation (*mĕn-strōō-ā′shŭn*). A normal discharge of blood from the vagina of an older girl or woman at monthly intervals.

Mesoderm (*mĕs′ō-dŭrm*). The middle of the three germ layers of cells from which the various parts of the body are formed.

Microscope (*mī′krō-skōp*). An instrument for making enlarged images of small objects.

Mixed breed. Same as *Hybrid*.

Navel (*nā′vĕl*). The scar that is left after the cord that attaches an unborn baby to its mother is severed. The umbilicus.

Nipple. The raised part of the breast from which the young sucks milk.

Nucleus (*nū'klē-ŭs*). The vital part of the cell.

Organ. A part of the body serving some particular purpose, as the heart, lungs, stomach.

Ovary (*ō'vă-rĭ*). The organ in the body of the female which produces the egg cells. (Plural, *ovaries.*)

Oviduct (*ō'vĭ-dŭkt*). The tube which discharges the egg cells in birds.

Ovum (*ō'vŭm*). The Latin word for egg. (Plural, *ova.*)

Oxygen (*ŏk'sĭ-jĕn*). A vital and necessary part of air.

Pelvis (*pĕl'vĭs*). The basket of bone bounded by the hip bones which contains the reproductive system, the bladder, and the lower part of the large intestine.

Penis (*pē'nĭs*). The organ or part of the male body which discharges (1) the urine or fluid waste and (2) the sperm fluid.

Pigment (*pĭg'mĕnt*). Coloring matter, especially in the cells and tissues of animals and plants, as, for instance, skin pigment.

Placenta (*plă-sĕn'tă*). The mass of blood vessels which provide for the feeding or nourishment of the baby while it is growing in its mother.

Pregnancy (*prĕg'năn-sĭ*). The state of being pregnant; the period in which a baby is developing in the mother.

Pregnant (*prĕg'nănt*). A woman is said to be pregnant when the baby is growing in her.

Premature (*prē-mă-tūr'*). Before the proper time. A premature baby is one born too early.

Pure breed. A race or variety of animal or person produced by mating always between parents of the same kind, as a pure-blooded Indian.

Quadruplets (*kwŏd'rū-plĕts*). Four persons born of the same mother at the same time.

Quintuplets *(kwĭn'tū-plĕts).* Five persons born of the same mother at the same time.

Rectum *(rĕk'tŭm).* The lower part of the intestine which discharges the solid waste matter of the body.

Reproduction *(rē-prō-dŭk'shŭn).* The process of producing young.

Reproductive cells *(rē-prō-dŭk'tĭv).* The sperm and egg cells.

Scrotum *(skrō'tŭm).* The sac which hangs below the penis and carries the testicles.

Semen *(sē'mĕn).* The fluid which carries the sperm cells.

Seminal emission *(sĕm'ĭ-năl ē-mĭsh'ŭn).* A normal discharge of semen in older boys and men occurring unconsciously during sleep.

Seminal fluid. Same as *Semen.*

Seminal vesicle *(vĕs'ĭ-k'l).* A small sac in the vas deferens for the storage of seminal fluid.

Sense organs. Parts such as the eye, ear, and nose which transmit impressions to the brain.

Sex. That which distinguishes individuals as male or female.

Sextuplets *(sĕks'tū-plĕts).* Six individuals born of the same mother at the same time.

Siamese twins *(sī-a-mēz').* Identical twins joined at one point of the body.

Sperm cell. The male reproductive cell; called also a *spermatozoön* (plural, *spermatozoa*).

Spermatozoön *(spŭr-mă-tō-zō'ăn).* Same as *Sperm cell.*

Sterilize *(stĕr'ĭ-līz).* To free from germs.

Suture *(sū'tūr).* Membranous space between the margins of the bones of a baby's skull at birth.

Teat *(tēt).* The mouthpiece or nipple of the milk gland in animals.

Temperature. The degree of heat or cold.

Testes *(tĕs'tēz).* Same as *Testicles.* (Singular, *testis.*)

Testicles *(těs'tĭ-k'ls).* Two organs suspended in the scrotum or sac on the outside of the male which secrete the sperm cells; called also *Testes.*

Trait. A personal characteristic, such as a certain color of hair or quality of voice or talent for some art.

Triplets *(trĭp'lĕts).* Three persons born of the same mother at the same time.

Tubes. See *Fallopian tubes.*

Twins. Two persons born of the same mother at the same time.

Udder. A mammary or milk gland which has two or more teats or nipples.

Umbilical cord *(ŭm-bĭl'ĭ-kăl).* The cord which connects the mother and baby before the baby is born.

Urethra *(ū-rē'thră).* The tube which discharges urine in both the male and the female, and in the male the semen as well. In the male it lies within the penis.

Urinate *(ū'rĭ-nāt).* To discharge the fluid waste of the body.

Urine *(ū'rĭn).* The fluid waste of the body formed by the kidneys and discharged from the bladder through the urethra.

Uterus *(ū'tĕr-ŭs).* The sac in the mother's body in which the embryo develops.

Vagina *(vă-jī'nă).* The passageway leading from the uterus to the outside of the body; the birth canal.

Vas deferens *(văs dĕf'ĕ-rĕnz).* The thick-walled tube which carries the seminal fluid from the testes to the urethra.

Virile *(vĭr'ĭl).* Capable of producing young, also, manly.

Water sac. The sac filled with fluid in which the embryo develops.

Wet nurse. One who feeds at the breast, or supplies milk for, a baby that is not her own.

Womb. Same as *Uterus.*